"This generation needs to be connected to our heritage of faith. Paul King offers this link, in bite-size morsels that will whet your appetite for more. I encourage you to savor each story in this book."

Dr. Tim Elmore, president of Growing Leaders.com;
vice president of EQUIP

"Christians on a spiritual journey need a road map. Dr. King's *Moving Mountains* is just such a road map. It is filled with advice from the scouts who have made this pilgrimage before, and their experiences not only describe the landscape of faith but also warn us of possible pitfalls and dangers on our way. Safe journey!"

Dr. George Kurian, president of Encyclopedia Society;
editor of *The World Christian Encyclopedia*

"Paul King retells the stories of twelve people well-known for their emphases on the spiritual life, more than half of them true heroes of the faith. A powerful retelling, but with a special focus on the faith life of each. Plenty of inspiration here to trust God for the impossible in life and ministry."

Dr. J. Robertson McQuilkin, chancellor and
president emeritus, Columbia International University

"Considering that without faith it is impossible to please God, *Moving Mountains* is a welcomed reminder for the just who have been called to live by faith! These 'old landmarks'—tested and proven—will challenge your faith to new heights. *Moving Mountains* is a must read!"

Rev. Michael Durso, pastor,
Christ Tabernacle Church, Brooklyn

"Dr. Paul King's *Moving Mountains* is a much-needed reminder of our heritage as believers. Reaching back into history, Paul gives us insight into the faith of many of the anointed ministries of the past. Here is a book that merges the evangelical and charismatic streams. Also Paul singles out a faith principle that undergirded the life of each of these great leaders. I commend it to all who hunger for more of God."

Dr. Ron Phillips, author, *Awakened by the Spirit*; senior pastor,
Central Baptist Church, Hixson, Tennessee

"If Hebrews 11 is sometimes called the 'hall of faith,'" I would define *Moving Mountains* as a 'hall of hope.' Paul King intrigues us with eye-opening biographies from mountain-moving Christians of the past. They shared one chief characteristic above all: great hope in Jesus Christ to transform life's greatest challenges with Kingdom power. But Paul digs deeper. He helps us apply the dynamics they experienced to our daily walk with the One who wants to be 'King of the mountains' for us, too. These are stories that must be shared!"

David Bryant, president, PROCLAIM HOPE!

"Believers in each new generation must 'catch up on the past' or forfeit the blessings God entrusted to previous generations. In its frantic search for 'something new,' the church today is fast cutting loose from its historic moorings and abandoning its rich spiritual resources for weak human substitutes. The message of a book like this is just what we need to get us back on course."

Warren W. Wiersbe, author and international conference speaker; former pastor of Moody Church and director of Back to the Bible

"Welcome to the inner circle of Christ-lovers who were never heroes to themselves because they gave ultimate adoration to Jesus alone. Paul King has called a meeting of these wise, devoted servants, leaving one empty chair in the circle for you. So, come! Sit in the company of the committed, and feast on wind and fire."

Dr. Calvin Miller, author of The Singer Trilogy, *Walking with the Saints* and many other books; professor of divinity at Beeson Divinity School

"Worldly wisdom says that what we learn from history is that nobody learns from history. That is not true for triumphant Christians. History is His story, and contemporary believers are all standing on the shoulders of the spiritual giants so well documented in this wonderful book by Paul King. Their message will challenge and reshape your life."

Dr. Neil T. Anderson, founder and president emeritus of Freedom in Christ Ministries; former chair, Practical Theology Department, Talbot School of Theology, Biola University; author of *The Bondage Breaker*, *Victory over the Darkness*, *Living Free in Christ* and many other books

"So many believers today try to live the Christian life without any reference points. Yet if we stand back and look at history, we find that the lives of great Christians provide bright lights to help us on our journey. I am so glad that author Paul King has assembled such a notable collection of biographies into one volume. This is so much more than history. Because of the testimony they left behind, these beacons of faith will help you go deeper with God."

J. Lee Grady, editor, *Charisma* and *Ministries Today* magazines

# MOVING MOUNTAINS

Lessons in Bold Faith from Great Evangelical Leaders

## PAUL L. KING

**Chosen**
Grand Rapids, Michigan

Published by Chosen Books
A division of Baker Publishing Group
P.O. Box 6287, Grand Rapids, MI 49516-6287
www.chosenbooks.com

Printed in the United States of America

Library of Congress Cataloging-in-Publication Data
King, Paul L.
    Moving mountains : lessons in bold faith from great evangelical leaders / Paul L. King.
        p.      cm.
    Includes bibliographical references.
    ISBN 0-8007-9375-7 (pbk.)
    1. Faith—Christianity—History of doctrines—19th century. 2. Evangelicalism—His-
tory—19th century. 3. Faith—Christianity—History of doctrines—20th century. 4. Evangelicalism—History—20th century. I. Title.
BT771.3.K56 2004
280'.4'0922—dc22                                                                                      2004001309

Permission has been secured from the publishers of works not in the public domain from which
more than three hundred words have been quoted. Each of these works is fully documented in the
endnotes. These acknowledgments include the following: George Müller, *The Autobiography of George
Müller* (New Kensington, Pa.: Whitaker Books, 1984). Used by permission of the publisher. Lyle Wesley
Dorsett, *E. M. Bounds: Man of Prayer* (Grand Rapids: Zondervan, 1991). Used by permission of Lyle
Wesley Dorsett. Andrew Murray, *Divine Healing* (New Kensington, Pa.: Whitaker House, 1982). Used
by permission of the publisher.

The following material is used by permission of *Alliance Life*, formerly *The Alliance Weekly*, published
by The Christian and Missionary Alliance, 8595 Explorer Drive, Colorado Springs, Colo. 80920:
John A. MacMillan, "The Authority of the Believer in the Ephesian Epistle: Part 6," *Alliance Weekly*, 20
February 1932, 116; John A. MacMillan, "The Authority of the Believer in the Ephesian Epistle: Part
7," *Alliance Weekly*, 27 February 1932, 133; John A. MacMillan, "The Authority of the Rod," *Alliance
Weekly*, 18 May 1940, 314; John A. MacMillan, "The Authority of the Intercessor," *Alliance Weekly*, 23
May 1936, 326–27.

Christian Publications, Inc., has granted permission for reprinting material from the following books:
Reprinted from A. W. Tozer, *The Pursuit of God*, copyright © 1982, 1993 Christian Publications, Inc.;
A. W. Tozer, *Five Vows of Spiritual Power*, copyright © 1996 Christian Publications, Inc.; James L. Snyder, *In Pursuit of God: The Life of A. W. Tozer*, copyright © 1991 Christian Publications, Inc. Used by
permission of Christian Publications, Inc., 800.233.4443, <www.christianpublications.com>. Material
in Chapter 11 has been adapted from Paul L. King, *A Believer with Authority*, 38, 39, 61–64, 90, 91, 93,
94, 102–105, 109, 224 and 231, copyright © 2001 Christian Publications, Inc. Used by permission of
Christian Publications, Inc., 800.233.4443, <www.christianpublications.com>.

Dedicated to my parents,
John and Evadine King

# Contents

7

# Acknowledgments

People who made this book possible begin with my wife, Kathy, and my children, Sarah and Christopher, who have shared their suggestions and have been patient with me as I have been working away on my laptop. I have bounced ideas off the minds of pastor friends Jim Garrett and Bill Sullivan. My aunt Lois King, once a missionary to Angola, Africa, introduced me to the writings of Andrew Murray when I was a teenager. My parents and pastors introduced me to the writings of A. B. Simpson and A. W. Tozer. (My parents spent part of their honeymoon more than fifty years ago at a Pennsylvania camp meeting listening to Tozer preach.) One of my mentors who encouraged me to write on faith, Dr. Charles Farah, Jr., went to be with the Lord before I completed this work. Jane Campbell, acquisitions editor for Chosen Books, has expressed her enthusiasm for this book and has assisted in the publishing process. My greatest assistance has come through literary agent and friend Dr. Mark Roberts, who helped me to enhance and fashion my writing style and the structure of the book. I would also like to thank the publishers who have given me permission to quote large amounts of material from these great writers. I acknowledge these permissions on the copyright page.

# Introduction

Walking by faith has become controversial: Some claim health, wealth and prosperity as their spiritual right, while others consider the Word of Faith movement a heresy. How can we know what is true? Is there even such a thing as a "walk of faith"?

I have had many conversations with people involved in the Faith movement. Some have been wise, sound and stable, while others are quite immature and imbalanced. I have met many who, though sometimes misguided and mistaken in their beliefs and practices of faith, love the Lord and are godly, sincere and humble. Others, unfortunately, have been presumptuous, self-centered and unsound. Still others have been deeply wounded by bad experiences with faith teaching and practice.

I myself embraced the faith teaching in the early 1970s when a popular faith teacher, who was then a pastor in my denomination, came and spoke at the church where I was serving as youth pastor. I followed the faith teaching wholeheartedly until I studied the Bible in Hebrew and Greek and took a course in hermeneutics (principles of interpretation) at college. Then I realized that *some* of the faith leaders' teachings did not line up with sound interpretation of Scripture in the original languages. I also became sick and tried to claim healing in faith without medicine. But I only got sicker. When my claiming in faith did not work, I abandoned the faith teaching—in fact, I became critical and cynical toward faith teachers.

A few years later I was sick for several months and could not get well, even with medical care. My Christian doctor told me that he did not know why I was not getting better and suggested I seek the Lord. I did spend time in prayer, and the Lord showed me that I had not only discarded unsound faith teaching, but also sound teaching on faith, which kept me from having the faith to receive healing. I realized I had "thrown out the baby with the bath water." I thought, "Nothing else is working, so I am going to try confessing healing by faith for thirty days. Maybe there is something to this teaching." So daily, I began to make positive confessions of faith and healing. Within thirty days I was healed.

I did not find out until some time later that making confessions of faith was not merely taught by modern Faith leaders, but in some form was also practiced by great evangelical leaders like Charles Spurgeon, Andrew Murray, A. B. Simpson and others mentioned in this book. I discovered that *some* faith principles taught today really *are* valid. As I read more of the writings of these leaders, I found distinct differences from some of what is often taught today. However, I was startled that there were also striking similarities. The more I studied, the more clearly I understood which faith teachings are sound and which are not. I talked with one of my mentors, who himself had been a critic of modern faith teaching. He reminded me of a Latin phrase *abusus non tollet usus*, which means, "The abuse does not carry away or negate the use." Just because some faith teachings have been taken to an extreme, it does not follow that the teaching is totally wrong. Rather, one truth has been emphasized to the neglect or exclusion of another. The solution, then, is not to condemn the entire teaching but rather to separate the wheat from the chaff, the gold from the alloy.

Through my studies I have found that these great evangelical leaders taught and practiced a form of faith that is both strong and sound. I commend them to you to strengthen your faith.

# 1

# George Müller
## (1805–1898)
### Apostle of Faith

---

**Faith principle:**

*You can depend totally on God!*

---

From George Müller's diary—an urgent request and answered prayer:

> November 20, 1857. The boiler at the New Orphan House No. 1 leaked considerably. We thought that it would last through the winter, although we suspected that it was nearly worn out. For me to do nothing and say, "I will trust in God," would be careless presumption, not faith in God.
>
> The condition of the boiler could not be known without taking down the brickwork around it. What then was to be done? For the children, especially the young infants, I was deeply concerned that they would suffer for lack of warmth. But how were we to obtain heat?

The installation of a new boiler would probably take many weeks. Repairing the boiler was a questionable matter because of the size of the work. Nothing could be decided until the brick-chamber was at least partially removed. That would take days, and what was to be done in the meantime to find warm rooms for three hundred children?

At last I decided to open the brick chamber and see the extent of the damage. The day was set when the workmen were to come, and all the necessary arrangements were made. The heat, of course, had to be shut off while the repairs were going on.

After the day was set for the repairs, a bleak north wind set in, bringing the first really cold weather of the winter. The repairs could not be put off, so I asked the Lord for two things—that He would change the north wind into a south wind, and that He would give to the workmen a desire to work. I remembered how much Nehemiah accomplished in fifty-two days while building the wall of Jerusalem because "the people had a mind to work" (Nehemiah 4:6).

The memorable day came. The evening before, the bleak north wind still blew, but on Wednesday the south wind blew, exactly as I had prayed. The weather was so mild that no heat was needed. The brickwork was removed, the leak was soon found, and the repairmen set to work. About half-past eight in the evening . . . the manager said, "The men will work late this evening and come very early again tomorrow."

"We would rather, sir," said the foreman, "work all night."

Then I remembered the second part of my prayer— that God would give the men "a mind to work." By the next morning, the repair of the boiler was accomplished. Within thirty hours the brickwork was up again, and the fire was in the boiler. All the time, the south wind blew so mildly that there was not the least need for any heat.[1]

This entry was typical of George Müller's extraordinary life of faith. Known as "The Apostle of Faith," George Müller was the greatest model and catalyst of faith of the nineteenth century, and perhaps the twentieth.[2] Consider some of the highlights of his walk of faith. He believed, prayed for and received miraculous

- provision in drought;
- protection from fatal epidemics;
- faith to control weather;
- property and funding to establish several orphanages without asking for money;
- provision of food for thousands of orphans.

## Meet George Müller

Who was this giant of faith? A Prussian by birth, George Müller had a passion for souls. He emigrated to England to evangelize Jews, but his fervor for prayer and compassion for children stirred him, through God's leading, to establish an orphanage based on faith principles. That initial step of faith led to founding five orphanages where he cared for thousands of children over sixty years. His life and teaching highlighted sound and bold principles of biblical faith. He taught enduring understandings of Mark 11:24, of praying in faith for healing, and of claiming the promises of God for provision of needs and answers to prayer. Müller modeled a complete trust in God. His faith-filled living spurred great nineteenth-century Christian leaders to daring actions of faith:

- *Charles Spurgeon*, mentored personally by Müller, became the greatest preacher of his century. He

17

launched one of the first mega-churches, as well as charity works, orphanages and a ministry of healing, all based on Müller's faith principles. He regarded a day spent with Müller as a foretaste of heaven.

- *J. Hudson Taylor,* a friend of Spurgeon's, also mentored by Müller, pioneered faith missions by establishing the China Inland Mission.
- *C. T. Studd,* a famous cricket player who gave away all his fortune, likewise launched into faith missions, founding the World Evangelization Crusade.
- As a result of observing Müller's walk of faith, Episcopalian medical doctor *Charles Cullis* established faith conventions at Old Orchard, Maine, and promoted divine healing by faith.
- *A. B. Simpson* followed Müller's principles, was miraculously healed at one of Cullis' meetings and founded The Christian and Missionary Alliance to promote worldwide evangelization, holiness, healing and faith.
- *R. A. Torrey,* associate of Dwight L. Moody and dean of Moody Bible Institute, testified that he owed his walk of faith and power to the example of George Müller.

What can we learn from the life of this great man of faith? What were the principles of faith that sustained his life and ministry and influenced the lives of great evangelical leaders? Here are eight faith principles Müller learned and lived—which you can, too!

### Just Ask God

"What do you mean, 'Just ask God'?" some might say. "Why do I need to ask God? He knows my needs."

Müller would reply simply from Scripture, "You have not because you ask not" (James 4:2, my translation). Müller sought God in prayer about *everything*, and his experiences show the kinds of requests we can expect God will grant when we ask in faith.

## ASK GOD FOR PROVISION

During the summer of 1864 a severe drought plagued England. Fifteen cisterns that supplied water for the three orphan houses were empty, and nine wells and a spring were almost completely dry. They needed two to three thousand gallons of water daily to provide for the children. Müller prayed daily for rain, but there was no rain. However, the day before they would run out of water, God remarkably provided—a nearby farmer unselfishly offered water from a brook running through his fields, "and thus there was abundance until the rains replenished cisterns and wells."[3] Müller learned that God does not always provide in the way we expect, but He always provides.

## ASK GOD FOR PROTECTION

In the late 1860s an epidemic of scarlet fever, typhoid fever and smallpox broke out in Bristol and the surrounding area for three years, causing much suffering and death. Müller and his staff prayed for the health and protection of the children. During the whole three years, not a single instance of scarlet fever or typhoid fever occurred. About fifteen of the twelve hundred children contracted mild cases of smallpox, but after further intensified prayer no other child became sick. After only nine months every child was healthy.[4]

### ASK WITH EXPECTATION THAT GOD WILL ANSWER

In 1865 hurricane-force winds damaged the orphan houses, causing twenty holes in the roofs and breaking large panes of glass. This happened over a weekend, so that no repairs could be made for two days. Müller and his staff prayed to "the Lord of the wind and the weather . . . to protect the exposed property during the interval." The wind and rain ceased until the following Wednesday, when a heavy downpour prevented the workers from repairing the one remaining exposure in the roof. Providentially, no further damage was incurred when the downpour came, because the hole was on the south side of the roof, but the rain came from the north. Again Müller went to prayer, and again the rain stopped, enabling the workers to finish the repairs.[5]

### ASK GOD FOR FAITH

Many Christians, hearing of these exceptional answers to prayer, might say, "I don't have faith for these things." Müller would simply reply, "Ask God for faith," just as the man responded to Jesus, "I do believe; help my unbelief" (Mark 9:24, NASB). Müller believed faith is not automatically received or worked up by our own efforts. Rather, faith is given by God *as we ask for it.* Though some today insist we are not to pray for faith because we already have it, Müller gives this counsel based on James 1:17: "As the increase of faith is a good gift, it must come from God, and therefore he ought to be asked for this blessing."[6]

### *Trust God Alone*

Müller believed we must depend on God alone, not man, not our job, not even on our own faith: "God is not likely to bless anything that leads a believer to depend

20

more on himself or his circumstances than on the believing God."[7] A. T. Pierson, Müller's biographer and interim successor to Spurgeon, described Müller's faith walk as "an experience of habitual *hanging upon the unseen God* and nothing else."[8] "Living by faith in God alone keeps my heart in perfect peace," Müller testified.[9]

What is particularly unique about Müller is that he never asked people for money, nor did he advertise his financial needs. Rather, he would ask God to impress upon someone's heart to give. Müller asserted:

> If anyone desires to live a life of faith and trust God he must not merely *say* that he trusts in God, but *really do so*. . . . I do not say it is wrong to make known our financial situation, but it hardly displays trust in God to expose our needs for the sake of getting other people to help us. God will take us at His word. If we trust in Him, we must be satisfied to stand with Him alone.[10]

Throughout his life he and his wife faithfully practiced this principle as an example to other Christians.

Through the decades, George Müller day by day sought God alone for the physical needs of the children. On several occasions, he was penniless to the very day or even hour of need—yet God always supplied. Only once in sixty years, Müller recalled, did he need to delay eating for half an hour before the food was supplied. "Not one, or five times, or five hundred times, but thousands of times in these threescore years have we had in hand not enough for one more meal, either in food or funds; but not once has God failed us; not once have we or the orphans gone hungry or lacked any good thing."[11] Müller did not always know how God was going to provide, but he had confidence God would provide.

## Establish a Positive Attitude Daily through the Word and Worship

Does our attitude affect our faith? Müller believed so. To Müller, renewing and strengthening this positive attitude of the inner man daily is a prerequisite to witnessing and helping others in the right spirit: "I saw more clearly than ever that the first great and primary business to which I ought to attend every day was to have my soul happy in the Lord."[12] He accomplished this by establishing a habit of walking, praying and meditating on the Word of God before breakfast each morning. Considering it nourishment for the inner man, Müller claimed this practice was also beneficial to his health. Living to the age of 92, he indeed did become healthier the older he became. After forty years of this faith walk he testified, "I cannot tell you how happy this service makes me. Instead of being the anxious, careworn man many persons think me to be, I have no anxieties and no cares at all. Faith in God leads me to roll all my burdens upon Him."[13]

## Saturate Your Mind and Spirit with the Word of God

Müller not only spent hours in prayer but also hours studying Scripture in its original languages of Hebrew and Greek. While some fear that education and scholarly study weaken faith, for Müller, intellectual rigor and piety went hand in hand. Müller is a clear-cut example of one whose faith was strengthened, not weakened, through scholarship. Early in his ministry, when he was engaging in Jewish evangelism, he studied twelve hours a day, mostly Hebrew, memorizing large portions of the Hebrew Old Testament. As a pastor in the early Brethren movement his preaching was expositional, often verse by verse, based on his in-depth studies in the original languages. Müller became a great man of faith *because* he studied the Word of God intensely and saturated himself with it. But Müller did not just study and memorize Scripture. He also meditated upon the Word of God and prayed over it. Following the practice of evangelist George Whitefield, he made it his habit to read the Scriptures on his knees. Believing that Jesus Christ is the same yesterday, today and forever (see Hebrews 13:8), he would pray the Scriptures, "turning the promises of God into a prayer and the prayer into a prophecy."[14] Sometimes he spent a whole week seeking the Lord in prayer and ruminating over the Word before claiming a promise from God. He thus combined intellectual pursuit with intimate fellowship with God, resulting in a faith that was both strong and sound.

### *Expect God to Use Your Trials to Feed Your Faith*

Müller speaks out of his wealth of experience when he proclaims, "The only way to learn strong faith is to endure great trials."[15] To Müller, "Trials are the food of faith."[16] Even in tough times he persevered, claiming, "We are never losers from doing the will of the Lord."[17] During an especially difficult trial in 1846, it appeared that, due to unknown obstacles and delay of funds, he would lose a parcel of land he had claimed from the Lord for an orphanage. Even though he had miraculously obtained a contract for the land at a great price four months earlier, the deal was about to fall through. In the midst of this struggle he wrote, "Our heavenly Father never takes anything away from His children unless He means to give them something better."[18] As it turned out, within a month the obstacles fell away and, just at the most critical time, he received more than £2,000.

In June 1835 both Müller's father-in-law and his infant son Elijah died just days apart and were buried in the same grave. Though the Müllers sensed the comfort and strength of the Lord, Müller went through a period of illness, probably as a result of grief and depression. Continuing about two months, the pain and weakness incapacitated him from doing any work or ministry, until one night God gave him grace to discipline himself to get up and kneel to pray when he just wanted to go to sleep. He testifies of his experience:

> No sooner had I begun to pray than His Spirit shone into my soul and gave me such a spirit of prayer as I had not enjoyed for many weeks. He graciously revived His work in my heart. I enjoyed that nearness to God and fervency in prayer for more than an hour. My soul had been panting for many weeks for this sweet experience. For the first time in this illness, I asked the Lord earnestly to restore me to health.[19]

Müller understood that God had to work something in his heart and restore his communion with God before he could ask for physical healing. Though he believed in God's healing power, he discerned that God may have a purpose for allowing the sickness, and a plan and timing for the healing to take place. He recognized that spiritual or emotional healing often precedes physical healing: At times, we need to *grow through* illness before being *delivered from* illness. Pierson describes Müller's response to severe illness:

> Sickness is often attended with strange self-disclosure. . . . As is often true in the history of God's saints, the sense of guilt, which seemed at first to have no root in conscience and scarce an existence, struck deeper into his being and grew stronger as he knew more of God and grew more like Him. . . . The more we live in God and unto God, the

more do our eyes become enlightened to see the enormity and deformity of sin, so that we recognize the hatefulness of sin more distinctly. . . . As godliness increases, the sense of ungodliness becomes more acute. . . . He so delighted in the will of God as to be able from his heart to say that he would not have his disease removed until through it God had wrought the blessing it was meant to convey. And when his acquiescence in the will of God had become thus complete he instinctively felt that he would speedily be restored to health.[20]

Müller also believed that trials taught spiritual lessons. In September 1838 he had been waiting on the Lord to supply money for rent, but the deadline when the rent was due, September 29, passed. The money *was* supplied three days later. When he asked the Lord why the money had not come in on time, the Lord showed him he should have been saving up rent money daily or weekly as God supplied it, rather than presuming God would bring it in all at once.

### Get the Leading of the Lord

Müller did not just ask God for something without first asking the Lord if he should even ask for that need. He wanted to be confident it was God's will to ask before asking in prayer. He asked the Lord for money only after he had a "leading from the Lord" to ask. Before claiming property to be a new orphan home in November 1835, he spent a week in prayer, repeatedly examining his motives. He received a strong assurance a week later and confidently asked the Lord for a building, £1,000 for expenses and people to run it. Within a month he received a gift of £100, and the promise of a house to use, but mostly the money came in only a few shillings at a time. Yet by the time of the opening in April 1836 everything was provided. Through this and other experiences Müller learned four key lessons about discerning God's leading, which we can benefit from today.

### WAIT ON THE LORD

Müller's policy was to wait on the Lord for four things: "First, to know whether a work is *God's* work; second, to know whether it is *my* work; third, to know whether it is God's time; fourth, to know whether it is God's way."[21] If Müller could not answer all four affirmatively, he concluded the Lord was not leading him to ask and believe for that request.

### USE SPIRIT-ENLIGHTENED REASONING

Müller was very practical in seeking the will of God, using what might be called "sanctified judgment." After establishing several orphan homes on the same street, he was facing the need for growth. As he sought God about relocating and building, he listed the pros and cons and reasoned out the issue:

> I was very busy that week and scarcely had time to consider it further. On Monday morning, however, I set apart some hours for prayerful consideration of the subject. I wrote down the reasons which appeared desirable that the Orphan Houses should be *moved* from Wilson Street, and the reasons *against moving.*
>
> . . . After I had spent a few hours in prayer and consideration of the subject, I began to see that the Lord was leading me to build.[22]

He practiced this method of decision-making on many other occasions as well, expecting the Lord to guide his reasoning.

## GET CONFIRMATION FROM OTHERS

Müller did not trust, however, that his own reasonings or impressions were automatically from the Lord. In addition, on this and other occasions he sought and received confirmation from several fellow workers in the church. Then he prayed each morning with his wife, asking God "for clearer light concerning the details of the project."[23] Receiving assurance, he would then proceed to ask for provision.

## DO NOT PRESUME UPON GOD

Müller believed he needed to step out and act on faith when God gave it, but *only* when God gave it: "Every new step was taken with care and prayer, that it should not be in the energy of the flesh, or in the wisdom of man, but in the power and wisdom of the Spirit."[24] On one occasion a blood vessel broke in his stomach, causing a severe hemorrhage. Though weak from the loss of blood, by the grace of God he preached the next morning, commenting, "The Lord gave me faith to get out of bed. I would consider it great presumption if the Lord had not given me the faith to do it."[25]

Can believers name and claim anything they desire, as some assert, according to Mark 11:24, Müller's prime faith Scripture? Only when they get a clear word or assurance of faith from God, Müller would advise. R. A. Torrey tells of his experience as a young Christian of misinterpreting this Scripture, as so many people do, and then how he learned from Müller's example:

> Here is the point at which I went astray in my early prayer life. Not long after my conversion I got hold of this promise of our Lord Jesus in Mark 11:24. . . . I said to myself, "All that I need to do if I want anything is to ask God for it and then make myself believe that I am

going to get it, and I'll have it." So whenever I wanted any thing I asked God for it and tried to make myself believe I was going to get it, but I didn't get it, for it was only "make believe," and I did not really believe at all. But later I learned. . . . George Müller never prayed for a thing just because he wanted it, or even just because he felt it was greatly needed for God's work. When it was laid upon George Müller's heart to pray for anything, he would search the Scriptures to find if there was some promise that covered the case. Sometimes . . . for days before he presented his petition to God. And when he found the promise, with his open Bible before him and his finger upon that promise, he would plead that promise and so he received what he asked.[26]

### Keep on Praying and Praising Until God Gives Assurance

Is it a lack of faith to ask God for something more than once? To those who say one should ask only once, George Müller counters, "We might as well say there is no need to tell Him once, for He knows beforehand what our need is. He wants us to prove that we have confidence in Him, that we take our place as creatures before the Creator."[27] He remarked that he had prayed for some things *thousands* of times over several years before receiving answers. As a student of Greek, he understood that the verbs in Matthew 7:7 express ongoing action: "Ask and keep on asking . . . seek and keep on seeking . . . knock and keep on knocking. . . ."

Regardless of how long he prayed, when Müller received assurance from God he knew it was time to begin praising Him:

I asked a thing once of God, which I knew to be according to His mind, and though I brought it day by day and generally many times a day before Him, in such assurance as to be able to thank Him hundreds of times for the answer before it was received, yet I had to wait three years and ten months before the blessing was given to me. At another time I had to wait six years; and at another time eleven and a half years. In the last case I brought the matter about twenty thousand times before God, and invariably in the fullest assurance of faith, and yet eleven and a half years passed before the answer was given.[28]

If God gives assurance, our praying can turn into praising even if the answer is not manifest.

## Believe and Use Biblical Financial Wisdom

Müller was an astute businessman as well as a man of faith and prayer. In addition to these universal concepts of faith he also practiced sound, successful financial principles based on Scripture and his faith walk. Here are four key lessons Müller learned that join faith and biblical finances today.

### GIVE GENEROUSLY

Müller did not view tithing as mandatory for Christians but instead as the minimum basis of generosity. He and his wife practiced giving far above a tithe of their increase. He believed that the more we give, the more we can receive to enable us to give even more[29]—a concept expanded upon by Charles Spurgeon and expressed today in the motto "Give to get to give."

### ASK SPECIFICALLY

Müller would interpret James 4:2 to mean, "You have not *precisely* what you need because you asked not for *precisely* what you needed." Fuzzy prayers get fuzzy answers; explicit prayers get explicit answers. Müller prayed for exact sums of money, and over and over he would receive precisely what he asked for. For example, on one occasion he prayed for £1,000 in British currency, and was given a variety of sums from a mere shilling to a hundred pounds from numerous sources. When he added them all together, they totaled *precisely* the figure he requested. On another occasion he petitioned the Lord to stir people to contribute their time, as well as furniture and clothing for the orphans. Consequently, he obtained *precisely* all he needed. On top of all that, people gave food and volunteered to provide childcare, and one person even donated a house! The answers did not always come quickly, but he persevered with repeated specific petitions. He prayed daily regarding one specific need for nearly five months before the provision arrived.

### STAY OUT OF DEBT

Müller wrote:

> My wife and I never went into debt because we believed it to be unscriptural according to Romans 13:8, "Owe no man anything, but to love one another." Therefore we have no bills with our tailor, butcher, or baker, but we pay for everything in cash. We would rather suffer need than to contract debts. Thus, we always know how much we have, and how much we can give away. Many trials come upon the children of God on account of not acting according to Rom. 13:8. . . . There is no promise that He will pay our debts.[30]

Charles Spurgeon, J. Hudson Taylor, A. B. Simpson, C. T. Studd and Amy Carmichael all maintained debt-free ministries as a result of Müller's influence. Bill Gothard's Institute in Basic Life Principles is a contemporary example of a ministry that has successfully practiced Müller's principles of staying out of debt and trusting God alone.

### EXAMINE YOUR MOTIVES

Müller believed God wants to provide abundantly for His children. He cautioned, however, about hindrances to receiving God's supply, such as a selfish attitude or motive for wanting to prosper:

> Suppose such a person had heard the promises about prayer, and should say, "Now I will try if these things are true, and I will ask God to give me a hundred thousand pounds sterling, and then I can give myself easy days; I can travel about and enjoy myself." Suppose he prays every day for this large sum of money, will he obtain it? Assuredly not! Why not? He does not ask for it that he may help the poor abundantly; that he may contribute to the work of God more liberally, but he asks that he may spend his life in idleness, and in enjoying the pleasures of the world.[31]

In other words, if a person asks God for prosperity for his own pleasure because he is a King's Kid, he is not in the will of God. But if he is praying that he may prosper for the sake of others, that is in accordance with God's desire.

Müller counsels us to take personal inventory of our lives:

> Have you ever considered that the very reason your earnings are so small may be because you spend everything on yourself? If God gave you more, you would only use it to increase your own comfort instead of looking to see who is sick or who has no work at all that you might help them. . . . The moment someone begins to give for the sake of receiving more back from the Lord, or he stops

sowing bountifully in order to increase his own possessions, the river of God's bounty will no longer flow.[32]

## Müller's Faith Can Be Yours!

You may be wondering, "How can I possibly live
Müller's faith?" Müller believed every Christian can grow
the same kind of faith he lived by. You can turn a small
measure of God-given faith into everyday faith. How?
Müller would encourage you just to exercise the faith
you already have and ask God to expand your faith. As
you act obediently in faith, God will grant you greater
faith. Müller remarked about his growth in faith:

> The first germ of faith in the soul is very much like a
> new-born infant in the cradle, very small and very weak,
> and its future growth and increase of strength as much
> depend on its daily constant exercise, as does the phys-
> ical development of the child. . . . I can now as easily
> trust God for thirty-five thousand pounds as I could at
> first for five thousand.[33]

Actually, early in his ministry Müller began by praying
for £40—and God supplied £50. That encouraged him to
pray and believe for £1,000 to establish the first orphan
house. His faith to believe God for greater provision
mushroomed through the years.

Müller wanted people to understand that the faith he
exercised is available for every believer:

> The faith which I am able to exercise is God's own gift. He
> alone supports it, and He alone can increase it. Moment
> by moment, I depend on Him. If I were left to myself,
> my faith would utterly fail. My faith is the same faith
> which is found in every believer. It has been increasing
> little by little for the last twenty-six years. . . .

I give the glory to God alone that He has enabled me to trust in Him, and He has not permitted my confidence in Him to fail. No one should think that my depending on God is an unusual gift given to me, which other saints have no right to expect. . . .

Do not let Satan deceive you into thinking that *you* could not have the same faith. When I lose something like a key, I ask the Lord to direct me to it; and I look for an answer to my prayer. When a person with whom I have made an appointment is late, and I am inconvenienced, I ask the Lord to hasten him to me. When I do not understand a passage of the Word of God, I lift up my heart to the Lord that He would, by His Holy Spirit, instruct me. I expect to be taught, although I do not fix the time and the manner it should be. When I am going to minister the Word, I seek help from the Lord. While I am conscious of my natural inability as well as utter unworthiness, I am confident and cheerful because I look for His assistance and believe that He will help me.

You may do the same, dear believing reader! Do not think that I am extraordinary or that I have privileges above God's other dear children. I encourage you to try it. Stand firm in the hour of trial, and you will see the help of God, if you trust in Him.[34]

That kind of faith can be yours!

## THINK AND DISCUSS

1. In what areas of your life do you need to depend more fully on God?
2. Which of Müller's principles of faith is the most helpful to you? Why?

3. Read Mark 11:19–24 and compare with John 14:12–13; 15:7; 1 John 5:14–15. When can we pray with confidence that God will answer our prayers?
4. How do you know when you have a leading from the Lord?
5. What are some of the ways you can exercise and increase your faith?
6. How do faith and financial wisdom work together?

## READ MORE ABOUT IT

George Müller, *The Autobiography of George Müller* (Springdale, Pa.: Whitaker Books, 1984)

Roger Steer, *Spiritual Secrets of George Müller* (Wheaton: Harold Shaw Publishers, 1985)

# 2

# J. Hudson Taylor
## (1832–1905)
### Pioneer of Faith Missions

---

**Faith principle:**

*Faith is a supernatural adventure.*

---

One morning young medical student James Hudson Taylor was dissecting a cadaver of a man who had died from a severe malignant fever. He worked slowly and carefully, knowing that the tiniest cut or scratch could cause him to become infected with the virus and die. Later in the morning he became weary, and then nauseous. By noon he had nearly fainted and was revived with a cup of water. Early in the afternoon his whole right side was filled with pain and he could not even hold a pencil to write. When Taylor described his symptoms to the teaching surgeon, the doctor replied that he must have scratched himself while performing the dissection. Taylor replied that he had not, but then recalled that he had pricked himself the night before with a sewing needle. The doctor replied that this was surely the reason for his pain. He advised Taylor to return home immediately and set his affairs in order, avowing, "You are a dead man!" The doctor warned that his strength would be sapped from him rapidly.

Taylor's first response was one of sadness that he would not be able to go to China as a missionary. But then a strong feeling rose up within him: "Unless I am greatly mistaken, I have work to do in China and shall not die." Rather than take a carriage to conserve his strength, he began to walk home. On the way he nearly fainted, so he took a carriage the rest of the way home. Upon arriving at home he washed his hand and pierced his finger to discharge the poisonous infection, and the pain became so intense he lost consciousness for a time. He survived the night, and after several weeks recuperating was out of danger, though still very weak. Two other students who had been infected at the same time had died, but he had survived. All through this time he had confidence from the Lord that he would live and go to China.

Still feeling exhausted and advised by the doctor to rest in the country, Taylor sensed an impression from the Lord to get up and walk two miles to his former place of employment. After further prayer and waiting on the Lord he was convinced this was what God wanted him to do. He asked the Lord for strength and then started to walk, discovering he was receiving strength for each step. When he came to a steep hill he paused and again asked the Lord for strength. After climbing the hill he had to stop and rest a while, but he completed his journey successfully, also climbing a staircase. The surgeon who advised him to stay in bed could not believe that he had been able to walk that distance, declaring, "Impossible! Why, I left you lying there more like a ghost than a man!" Taylor had opportunity to share the Gospel and his walk of faith with this skeptic. With tears in his eyes, the doctor responded, "I would give all the world for a faith like yours."[1]

## Meet J. Hudson Taylor

Such a faith, stirred by the example and principles of his friend George Müller, enabled James Hudson Taylor "to venture wholly on the Lord."[2] He lived, like Müller, a faith that risks:

- In 1863 he launched out on his own without organizational support, founding the China Inland Mission (today known as the Overseas Missionary Fellowship). This earned him the title of "Pioneer of Faith Missions."
- He gave away his last coin to a poor family whose wife was dying. Through his prayers, she recovered and the next day he received back from an anonymous source four times what he had given.
- When sailing for China, Taylor prayed twice for protection from shipwreck and saw God change the winds and calm a storm.
- Like Müller, he was often without food and finances until the last hour it was needed.
- He overcame criticism, physical illness, depression, persecution and loss of loved ones to become one of the greatest and most godly missionary leaders.

To J. Hudson Taylor, faith was a supernatural adventure. He claimed the Scripture that "Jesus Christ is the same yesterday and today, yes and forever" (Hebrews 13:8, NASB). Four decades later, out of his many experiences of life he continued to maintain, "We are a supernatural people born again by a supernatural birth, kept by a supernatural power, sustained on supernatural food, taught by a supernatural Teacher from a supernatural Book. We are led by a supernatural Captain in right paths to assured victories."[3] One writer described him as always walking "knee deep in miracles."[4] Taylor believed in and experienced the supernatural power of God to provide miraculous protection, calm storms, send rain in drought, bring healing to the dying and speak through words of prophecy.[5] Let us look at some of the principles and experiences of Hudson Taylor's supernatural adventure of faith.

### We Have a Supernatural Relationship—Be in Constant Communion with Christ

According to his son Howard Taylor, "the outstanding thing about Hudson Taylor's early experience was that he could not be satisfied with anything less than the best, God's best—the real and constant enjoyment of His presence. To go without this was to live without sunlight, to work without power."[6] Taylor believed, "The real secret of an unsatisfied life lies too often in an unsurrendered will."[7] At a young age Taylor surrendered himself to God as his Lord:

> Well do I remember how in the gladness of my heart I poured out my soul before God. Again and again confessing my grateful love to Him who had done everything for me, who had saved me when I had given up all hope and even desire for salvation, I besought Him to give me some work to do for Him as an outlet for love and gratitude. . . .
>
> Well do I remember as I put myself, my life, my friends, my all upon the altar, the deep solemnity that

came over my soul with the assurance that my offering was accepted. The presence of God became unutterably real and blessed, and I remember . . . stretching myself on the ground and lying there before Him with unspeakable awe and unspeakable joy. For what service I was accepted I knew not, but a deep consciousness that I was not my own took possession of me which has never been effaced.[8]

As a result of this encounter, Taylor coined the well-known expression, "Christ is Lord of all or He is not Lord at all."[9] From the point of that experience, he lived with a commitment to Jesus Christ as the Lord of *all* his life.

Drawing on Müller's faith principles, Hudson Taylor counseled, "How then to have our faith increased? Only by thinking of all that Jesus is and all He is for us: His life, His death, His work, He Himself as revealed to us in the Word to be the subject of our constant thought."[10] Along with other classic evangelical writers, he taught that a positive mental attitude will affect one's health and outcome of life—not by one's own mental effort but by dwelling on Jesus and His Word, and experiencing "the joy of unbroken communion."[11]

### We Are a Supernatural People—Exercise the Muscles of Faith

While we enhance our faith by discovering that it is Christ's work within us, that does not mean we have no role to play in increasing our faith. Hudson Taylor believed faith is a gift from God, but it grows by exercise of the "spiritual muscles of faith," which, he claimed, is impossible without trial. He taught the principle of growth "from faith to faith"; that is, to him who exercises the faith he has, more faith will be given.[12] Before leaving England for China he wanted to be sure he had the right kind of faith and sufficient faith to trust in God alone when he got to China. He knew he would not have others to depend on in China, realizing he would be "far from all human aid, there to depend upon the living God alone for protection, supplies and help of every kind." He believed he needed to exercise his muscles of faith, writing, "How important to learn, before leaving England, to move man through God by prayer alone."[13]

Taylor learned to do this through a significant incident in his life. His employer was late paying his salary. Taylor determined to ask God to remind his employer, but he would not remind his employer himself. He was down to his last half-crown coin. He encountered a poor man whose family was starving and his wife dying. He went to pray for the man's wife and struggled under heavy conviction about giving up his last coin. Finally, he did, and, as a result, his heart was filled with peace and joy, and the woman recovered. Before going to bed that night he reminded the Lord of the verse "He that hath pity upon the poor lendeth unto the LORD" (Proverbs 19:17), also requesting that the loan not be a long one, as he had nothing for dinner the next day. The next morning the mailman brought a letter from an unidentified source that contained a half-sovereign, four times as much as he had given away. He exclaimed, "Praise the Lord! Four hundred percent for twelve hours' investment—that is good interest!" Years later he remarked on the incident, "Then and there I determined that a bank that could not break should have my savings or earnings." He recalled this incident again and again in times of difficulty, for he learned that exercising his faith would increase his faith.[14]

From that point on, Taylor made it his practice to "claim God's supply from the bank of heaven." Whenever the mission got down to its last bag of food Taylor would remark, "Then the Lord's time for helping us must be close at hand." And sure enough, the provision always came. He had assurance in the faithfulness of God. Following the example of Müller, Taylor would not go into debt or let his needs be made known publicly, proclaiming the principle that "God's work done in God's way will not lack God's support. He is just as able to supply funds ahead of time as afterward and He much prefers doing so."[15]

### We Are Kept by a Supernatural Power—Trust in God's Providential Protection

In September 1853 Hudson Taylor set sail for China to fulfill the vision God had given him to reach the people of the Orient. Dangers arose even before the ship came to the ocean. For twelve days they were tossed about by hurricane-force winds through the channel between Ireland and Wales, in danger of being crushed on the rocks. The waters foamed, splashing over the sides of the ship onto the deck. The pitching of the boat from side to side made it difficult to stand. The captain proclaimed, "Unless God help us, there is no hope." Looking back on the crisis Taylor's son and biographer perceived that supernatural spiritual warfare was taking place: "It almost seemed as though the great enemy, 'the prince of the power of the air,' knowing of the possibilities enfolded in the life of one young life on board, was doing his utmost to send her to the bottom."[16] Though Taylor had maintained an attitude of joy and peace in the midst of the storm, at one point he felt forlorn and was driven to despair. He went below the deck, prayed and read a hymn, some psalms and John 13–15. The peace of the Lord came upon him and he fell asleep in the midst of the storm. When he awoke the weather had improved a little, but it then worsened again. As they were dangerously nearing the rocks Taylor was reminded of the Scripture "And call upon me in the day of trouble: I will deliver thee, and thou shalt glorify me" (Psalm 50:15). He bound some things together that would float, went up on deck and prayed one more prayer for God's deliverance. Just as they were about to crash on the rocks, the wind changed direction, and they were able to steer the ship clear. They gave praise for God's providential protection.[17]

Later on the same journey, when they neared the coast of New Guinea, just the opposite situation occurred. There was no wind and the boat became listless in the water, being swept by the current toward hidden reefs. After great efforts by the crew to steer the ship away from the reefs, the captain had given up, saying there was nothing else they could do. Taylor asserted to the captain, "Yes, there is. There are four of us who are Christians. Let us go and pray for a wind to come." The captain replied, "Go ahead." After a short but inspirational time of prayer, Taylor had confidence to stop praying and instructed the captain to hurry and put up the sail, for the wind was coming quickly. And sure enough, to the surprise of the captain and crew, the wind stirred up rapidly. In only minutes they were plowing through the sea at nearly seven knots![18]

These two remarkable but true stories are reminiscent of Paul's stormy voyage on the Mediterranean Sea on the way to Rome. Just as God protected and sustained the apostle and his fellow travelers, so God protected and sustained Hudson Taylor. Thus, the book of Acts was reenacted through Taylor's life in the nineteenth century.

An important lesson of faith Taylor learned was to trust in God fully, yet not presume upon Him. He had given away the life preserver his mother had given him, believing he needed just to trust God to preserve his life.

Later, though, when he tied together the floatable items, he felt no inconsistency or lack of faith, and on future voyages he always took along a life preserver. Reflecting upon the incident years later, he commented on the need for wisdom in the exercise of faith:

> I was a very young believer, and had not sufficient faith in God to see Him in and through the use of means. Ever since, I have seen clearly the mistake I made; a mistake that is very common in these days, when erroneous teaching on faith-healing does much harm, misleading some as to the purposes of God, shaking the faith of others, and distressing the minds of many. The use of means ought not to lessen our faith, and our faith in God ought not to hinder whatever means He has given us for accomplishment of His own purposes. . . . [T]o me it would appear as presumptuous and wrong to neglect the use of those measures which He Himself has put within our reach, as to neglect to take daily food, and suppose that life and health might be maintained by prayer alone.[19]

### We Are Led by a Supernatural God—Trust in God's Faithfulness

As a young missionary Taylor had faithfully served the Lord, but he often struggled with his faith—until he came into his deeper life experience of surrender to God, what people variously call the "crisis of sanctification" or "baptism in the Spirit." He called it "the exchanged life," in which he exchanged his weak, defeated life for Christ's life. He claimed Galatians 2:20, ". . . nevertheless I live; yet not I, but Christ liveth in me." At the height of his spiritual "dark night of the soul" a fellow missionary had written to him of his own experience, declaring, "But how to get faith strengthened? Not by striving after faith, but by resting in the Faithful One."[20] In that moment he discovered that faith is not a matter of struggling, not of working up faith, but resting—trusting peacefully and confidently in the faithfulness of God, and his life was transformed.

As a result, one of Hudson Taylor's favorite Scriptures became Mark 11:22, "Have faith in God." In fact, these words were engraved over the entrance to the China Inland Mission headquarters in London. He understood that in the original Greek it could be translated literally "Have the faith of God"; hence, his own preferred reading of the passage became, "Reckon on God's faithfulness." He explained, "I could not reckon on my faith but I could reckon on God's faithfulness."[21] He did not endeavor to have faith in his own faith but trusted in the very faith (or eternal faithfulness) of God Himself. His rendering "Reckon on God's faithfulness" became a popular motto, adopted by several other evangelical leaders such as Oswald Chambers, F. B. Meyer and F. F. Bosworth.[22]

### We Are Sustained by a Supernatural Food—Partake of the Word of God

Scripture was to Hudson Taylor as his daily bread, supernatural food that sustained him through all his activities, decision-making and crises. His faith rested in the promise of God regarding His Word: "It shall accomplish that which I please and . . . prosper in the thing whereto I sent it" (Isaiah 55:11). He possessed confidence that God's Word would have an effect.

He believed that the Scriptures were beyond human reasoning, that "superhuman wisdom" is needed to comprehend the Word of God: "Can feeble man expect to grasp divine power, or to understand and interpret the works or the providences of the All-Wise? And if not, is it surprising that His Word also needs superhuman wisdom for its interpretation? Thanks be to God, the illumination of the Holy Ghost is promised to all who seek for it: what more can we desire?"[23]

Taylor often prayed and studied the Scriptures by candlelight during the wee hours of the morning when he could be without distractions and the busyness of the day, even on his frequent travels. When he was about seventy years old he commented to one of his children, "I have just finished reading the Bible through today, for the fortieth time in forty years." Howard Taylor, with a quote from Andrew Murray, described his father's dependency upon Scripture as a way of life: "Let the Word create around you, create within you a holy atmosphere, a holy, heavenly light, in which your soul will be refreshed and strengthened for the work of daily life."[24]

### We Have a Supernatural Victory—Be an Overcomer

Taylor faced many challenges and trials throughout his ministry. He was assailed several times with physical illness, many times lacked funds and was severely criticized for his innovative methods. Four of his eight children died young, and his first wife, Maria, died at the age of 33. Some of his missionaries were attacked and killed, and mission property was destroyed. Not surprisingly, he suffered times of deep depression again and again throughout his life. Through it all, however, he rebounded with a positive attitude of faith. He proclaimed, "Satan, the Hinderer, may build a barrier about us, but he can never roof us in, so that we cannot look up."[25] One of his biographers noted, "Whether he was battling despair or floating on euphoric faith, Hudson Taylor drove himself—and the gospel—even deeper into China."[26]

Taylor experienced severe deprivations as a missionary, yet looking back over his years of ministry, amazingly he recalled, "I never made a sacrifice." What a selfless attitude he demonstrated! His personal outlook regarding prosperity was this:

> Having now the twofold object in view . . . of accustoming myself to endure hardness, and of economizing in order to help those among whom I was laboring in the Gospel, I soon found that I could live upon very much less than I had previously thought possible. . . . My experience was that the less I spent on myself and the more I gave to others, the fuller of happiness and blessing did my soul become.[27]

When someone cynically sniped that he must be living hand to mouth, he rejoined, "Yes, I suppose so. But it is God's hand to my mouth!"[28] Taylor understood the dangers of not depending totally on God and cautioned, "While the sun of prosperity shines upon me I may safely enjoy myself here without Him."[29]

Hudson Taylor testified of God's supernatural work in the midst of great adversity, recounting that he had

> seen God, in answer to prayer, quell the raging of the storm, alter the direction of the wind, and give rain in the midst of a prolonged drought . . . stay the angry passions and murderous intentions of violent men, and bring the machinations of His people's foes to naught . . . raise the dying from the bed of death, when all human aid was vain . . . preserve from the pestilence that walketh in the darkness, and from the destruction that wasteth at noonday.[30]

## You, Too, Can Join This Adventure of Faith!

Hudson Taylor provides a model for us of one who overcame great difficulties through his faith in God. He observed out of his life experiences, "I have found that there are three stages in every great work of God: first, it is impossible, then it is difficult, then it is done."[31]

Andrew Murray summed up the effect of the ministry of Hudson Taylor:

> Under the leadership of one man of faith, God had, in the course of thirty years, led out 600 missionaries into the field, without any guarantee of funds for their support beyond what God might give in answer to believing prayer. . . .
>
> Hudson Taylor's experience shows us how God trains a man to believe in Him, to wait on Him, to give himself up entirely to His will and service, however great the difficulty may be. . . .
>
> God had set forth Hudson Taylor as an example of what He can do for a young man who gives himself wholly to live by faith in God as he seeks to do God's work. . . .
>
> How can every believer be trained for this? The lesson is very clear. We have seen the path in which the power of believing prayer came to him. He gave himself wholly to God's work; this gave him the confidence that God would care for him and all his work. Faith cannot grow strong except by exercise. Difficulties are the proving ground of faith; they give it nourishment and strength.[32]

Hudson Taylor's life motto was straightforward, yet filled with faith and power: "There is a living God. He has spoken in His Word. He means what He says. And He is willing and able to perform what He has promised."[33] Taylor's simple yet profound creed can lead *you* into a supernatural adventure of faith!

## THINK AND DISCUSS

1. How can you enhance your relationship and fellowship with Christ? Is there an area of your life in which you have not given Him full Lordship?

2. In what ways are the muscles of your faith being exercised and stretched? In what ways can you strengthen your faith muscles?
3. How do you balance stepping out in faith with not acting in presumption upon the Lord?
4. How do you reconcile resting in faith with the struggle of spiritual warfare?
5. In what practical ways can you be nourished in your faith by the Word of God?
6. What obstacles do you need to overcome? What Scripture verses or chapters encourage and strengthen your faith?
7. Which of Taylor's principles of faith is the most helpful to you? Why?

## READ MORE ABOUT IT

### Biographical

Howard and Geraldine Taylor, *Hudson Taylor's Spiritual Secret* (Chicago: Moody Press, 1932)
Phyllis Thompson, *Hudson Taylor: God's Venturer* (Chicago: Moody Press)

### Book by Hudson Taylor

*Union and Communion with Christ* (Minneapolis: Bethany House Publishers)

# 3

# Charles H. Spurgeon
## (1834–1892)
### Prince of Faith Preachers

---

**Faith principle:**

*You can grow great faith
that overcomes life's challenges.*

---

In 1855 a life-threatening cholera plague swept through London, England. Thousands of people were dying, as many as two thousand a week. Young Baptist pastor Charles Spurgeon had buried many members of his congregation. In deep depression he wrote to his father, "Lost three [church members] on Sunday last. . . . I do not know how to keep from constant weeping—when I see others die." By running all over London trying to visit the sick and dying and comfort the families who had lost loved ones, he suffered both physically and emotionally from sheer exhaustion and lack of sleep. As a result, he fell into intense despair and, having been exposed to all the diseased people to whom he had ministered, even feared for his own life.

One day, after yet another funeral, he wandered down a street despondently, wondering how he was ever going to make it. He passed by a pharmacy and noticed a poster in the window, placed there by the Christian owner. On the sign appeared the words of Psalm 91:9–10: "Because thou hast made the LORD, which is my refuge, even the most High, thy habitation; there shall no evil befall thee, neither shall any plague come nigh thy dwelling."

As the dejected young pastor pondered those words of Scripture, and repeated them again and again, through the Spirit of God faith arose within him, dissipating his sense of hopelessness and fear. He claimed these words as his own and went about his work in peace and confidence that God would keep him safe. He sang the words of the old hymn, "Not a single shaft can hit, till the love of God sees fit," and adopted Oliver Cromwell's motto as his own, "Man is immortal until his work is done." As a result of his confessions of faith, he escaped the plague's grasp and his depression turned into joy.[1]

## Meet Charles Haddon Spurgeon

This is but one of many examples of the overcoming faith of Charles Spurgeon. Known as the "Prince of Preachers" of the nineteenth century, the famous Baptist pastor preached and lived a life of extraordinary faith. Spurgeon maintained a close friendship with both George Müller and Hudson Taylor, his older mentors. When as a young man he first met Müller, Spurgeon responded with awe, "I could not speak a word for the life of me," and called him "that heavenly man."[2] Spurgeon, Müller and Taylor promoted one another's ministries through prayer, financial giving, personal support and involvement. The three of them became a powerful triad of faith in the nineteenth century. Their impact has spilled over into the twentieth century and continues into the twenty-first. Some of Spurgeon's great accomplishments of faith include the following:

- Pastored one of the first megachurches of six thousand members.
- Impacted thousands of Christian leaders through his sermons for over a century.
- Set up orphanages and a pastors' college by using the same faith principles as Müller.
- Believed in and experienced supernatural revelations.
- Carried on a ministry of prayer, bringing healing to thousands, even while sick himself.
- Trained nearly a thousand ministers through his pastors' college.
- Overcame chronic pain and repeated bouts of depression.

What kind of faith empowered Spurgeon's ministry? Along with the principles practiced by his friends, he taught and modeled the following main beliefs.

### Believe in Continuing Supernatural Power

Although at one time Charles Spurgeon did not believe that miracles still happen today, he came to believe, like his friend J. Hudson Taylor, in the operation of the supernatural power of the Spirit:

If at the commencement of the gospel we see the Holy Spirit work great signs and wonders, may we not expect a continuance—if anything, an increased display—of His power as the ages roll on? . . . If there is not a miraculous spiritual power in the church of God today, the church is an imposter. . . . Only let men come back to the real gospel and preach it ardently, not with fancy words and polished speech but as a burning heart compels them and as the Spirit of God teaches them to speak it; then will great signs and wonders be seen. We must have signs following; we cannot otherwise answer the world.[3]

Belief in supernatural gifts was not theory for Spurgeon, for he was also personally acquainted with, and had even himself experienced, supernatural words of knowledge, dreams and visions, prophecy and healing.[4] He understood the reality of spiritual warfare, for his grandfather James Spurgeon, also a great man of faith, recounted a vivid dream in which he was accosted by the devil.[5] One man, after receiving prayer from Spurgeon, dreamed that Jesus appeared to him, assuring him that the demons had been cast out.[6] Charles Spurgeon himself recounted that occasionally he received revelation from God through a dream.[7] He testified to the reality of the gift of prophecy, as a preacher by the name of Richard Gill prophesied over him when he was ten years old (even before his conversion), declaring, "This child will one day preach the gospel, and he will preach it before multitudes."[8]

Spurgeon himself operated under a prophetic anointing, exercising upon occasion what some might today call a "word of knowledge." As a young preacher, for example, an older minister rebuked him in a meeting, snidely implying that Spurgeon was a young, impudent upstart. Spurgeon received a revelation from God, responding that "a minister, having fallen into open sin, had disgraced his calling and needed to go into seclusion . . . till his character had to some extent been restored."

Unknown to Spurgeon, but known to many in the meeting, this man had indeed fallen into open sin.[9] Thus, the man was shamed and Spurgeon was supernaturally vindicated.

On another occasion, in the middle of a sermon Spurgeon received a word from God and declared, "There is a man sitting here, who is a shoemaker; he keeps his shop open on Sundays, it was open last Sunday morning. He took in nine pence and there was a four pence profit; he sold his soul to Satan for four pence." The man was indeed in the congregation, and immediately he surrendered his life to Christ. In yet another sermon he stated that a young man wearing gloves he had stolen from his employer was in the meeting. And yes, there was such a man present. He came and confessed all. According to Spurgeon's biographer, dozens were converted through similar incidents.[10] Many today would call these occurrences "power encounters."

Unknown to most Christians today, Spurgeon had a tremendous ministry of healing. His original biographer, Baptist pastor and theologian Russell Conwell, declared the year after his death, "No man probably, in England or America, in this century, has healed so many people as Mr. Spurgeon."[11] He devoted an entire chapter to several examples out of the thousands of healings that occurred in Spurgeon's ministry. Though he himself said he was unworthy of possessing the gift of healing,[12] Spurgeon would thus today be considered in the ranks of a Kathryn Kuhlman or an Oral Roberts.

Although Spurgeon read volumes about healing, he did not derive a definitive theology of healing. Unlike some today who try to box God into specific formulas for faith and healing, he always left room for the mysteries and sovereignty of God. Some people for whom he prayed were healed immediately; others over time. Still others grew worse and died. He never received healing of his painful gout and Bright's disease, nor was his wife, Susanna, ever healed of her semi-invalid state. Some might invalidate his healing ministry on that basis, but it did not keep Spurgeon from believing that God does heal, nor did it prevent him from continuing to pray for others with miraculous results. He would encourage us to pray in faith and trust God to work in His own way and time.

### Develop Faith as Spiritual Sensitivity to God

Key to his supernatural insight and power, Spurgeon possessed a rare spiritual sensitivity to the voice of God and the things of the Spirit. He understood faith to operate by spiritual senses:

> The natural man has eyes, but by faith we see Him who is invisible. The natural man has his hand and his feeling. We live not by feeling, but our faith is the hand by which we take hold upon eternal realities. The natural man has his ear and is delighted with sweet sounds, but our faith is the ear through which we hear the voice of God and sometimes catch stray notes from the harps of the angels.[13]

Spurgeon walked closely with God and developed a keen awareness of His still, small voice. He also developed spiritual discernment, acknowledging that human senses can sometimes be deceiving, giving indicators contradictory to spiritual senses.

Spurgeon's great faith and his power in preaching arose out of his close communion with God. "Spend much time alone with Jesus," he testified, "and you will have much assurance. Spend little time alone with Jesus, and your faith will be shallow, polluted with many doubts and fears, and lacking in the joy of the Lord."[14] Speaking of his own devotional life, Spurgeon explained, "Faith has the daily practice of pleading promises with

God, speaking to Him face to face as a man speaks to his friend, and receiving favors from the right hand of the Most High."[15] Such an intimate relationship with his heavenly Father gave him great confidence to pray with faith and expect God to grant his requests.

## Get Your Faith from Christ Himself

Since faith is nurtured in fellowship with Christ, Spurgeon emphasized that He is the *source* of our faith. To Spurgeon, Jesus is the one ultimate magnetic force who draws us to Himself.[16] Similar to the contemporary idea of exercising faith through a point of contact, he explains that faith brings a person into "vital contact with Christ" like an electrical current.[17] Speaking of the woman who touched the hem of Jesus' garment, Spurgeon called her action "faith in its 'touch.'"[18] We activate our faith by being in touch with Christ, and at the same time acting by faith turns on the switch to God's power.

Spurgeon also stressed that Christ also must be the *object* of our faith: "It must be faith in the finished work of Christ; you must have no confidence in yourself or any man, but rest wholly and entirely upon Christ, else your shield will be of no use."[19] He further explained, "When you have no faith in yourself, there is more room in the soul for faith in Jesus."[20] He warned those who would make an icon or idol of their faith, exhorting that faith should not be exalted "above the divine source of all blessing which lies in the grace of God. Never make a Christ out of your faith. . . . Our life is found in 'looking unto Jesus' (Hebrews 12:2), not in looking to our own faith. By faith all things become possible to us, yet the power is not in the faith but in the God in whom faith relies."[21] He would object to the idea of having faith in your own faith or that healing can take place by faith without God's intervention. Spurgeon admonished,

"Your faith must be of heaven's forging, or your shield will certainly fail you."[22]

## Tap into God's Power Forces of Faith and Prayer

On the basis of understanding that Christ is the source of our faith, Spurgeon believed that faith is a powerful spiritual force from the very nature and heart of God that "has taken possession of the inner battery and can send the sacred current of His life to every part of our nature."[23] He recognized that the linkage of prayer and faith acts like a powerful electrical force from God, and he described the prayer life of his church as the "heavenly electricity of believing prayer."[24] On one occasion he led a group of people to the basement of Metropolitan Tabernacle to show them its "power plant"—a group of about three hundred people on their knees praying! Many people for whom Spurgeon prayed personally experienced his faith and prayers as a powerful force, even feeling impulses, "mysterious impressions" or "strange sensations" like trembling, heat, chills or electricity flowing through their bodies.[25]

While acknowledging that faith could not be squeezed into a formula, as some do today, Spurgeon taught that God established laws to "govern nature and direct providence."[26] He believed that faith and prayer operate by such laws: "Perhaps there are other forces and laws that He has arranged to bring into action just at the times when prayer also acts—laws just as fixed and forces just as natural as those that our learned theorizers have been able to discover. The wisest men do not know all the laws that govern the universe."[27] Such faith, claimed Spurgeon, "creates peace and joy" and "is full of inventions."[28] For Spurgeon, faith was a creative force of healing, protection and salvation.

Some today view faith or even the Holy Spirit as a mere influence or an impersonal force, but this is not what Spurgeon meant. For Spurgeon, faith was a part of the very nature of God. Others believe that unbelievers and believers alike can tap into a natural law of faith and manipulate the force of faith. On the contrary, he would say that they have failed to discern between the soulish or natural use of faith as a force, and the Spirit-led use of faith as a force. According to Spurgeon, God must redeem and transform natural faith. Much of what some call developing one's faith, and using the law of faith as a force, may in reality be soul-force rather than from the Holy Spirit.

He also viewed prayer as a great powerful force, "coercing the universe, binding the laws of God themselves in fetters."[29] There is a sense in which our prayers do spur God to act on our behalf. When we are walking close to God, Spurgeon asserts that prayer is able to prevail with Him. However, Spurgeon did not mean that God is bound by our prayers. On the contrary, this prayer must spring from faith imparted by Him—again, God as the source of faith.

### Faith Acts on Knowing Who We Are in Christ

Spurgeon asserted that the promises of blessing in Deuteronomy 28 are available to the believer today. Referring to Deuteronomy 28:13, "The LORD shall make you the head and not the tail, and you only shall be above, and you shall not be underneath" (NASB), Spurgeon declares, "Though this be a promise of the law, it stands good for the people of God; for Jesus has removed the curse, but He has established the blessing. It is for saints to lead the way among men by holy influence; they are not to be the tail, to be dragged hither and thither by others. . . . Are we not in Christ made kings to reign upon the earth?"[30] He understood the importance of knowing who we are in Christ and exercising faith from our exalted position in Christ. On one occasion when he was experiencing intense pain, he cried out to the Lord, "pleading his sonship" as a child of the heavenly Father. Within a few moments the pain subsided and he fell asleep peacefully.[31]

Throughout his life Spurgeon suffered many attacks on his character and his ministry. In the midst of the harassments he prayed Isaiah 54:17, "We will stand on Your promise, 'No weapon that is formed against thee shall prosper.'"[32] He found victory and vindication through claiming these promises of God. Spurgeon encourages us today, "What innumerable gifts faith has already bought us. It is as though a key has been given to God's storeroom and we are allowed to feast upon all that the Lord has prepared for them that love Him. To know the privilege of heirship with Christ, does not this bind you fast to your Elder Brother?"[33]

Like his friends Müller and Taylor, Spurgeon believed we have the right and privilege to bank on God's promises, expanding on the concept of "the bank of heaven":

> Some bank bills require the signature of the person for whom they are drawn, and they would not be payable at the bank, though regularly signed, unless countersigned by the person to whom they are due: now many of the Lord's promises are drawn in like fashion. Armed with such promises, you go to the bank of prayer, and you ask to have them fulfilled, but your petitions are not granted because they need to be countersigned by the sign-manual of your faith in them; and when God has given you grace to believe his promise, then shall you see the fulfillment of it with your eyes.[34]

### You Can Grow Your Faith by Exercising It

Spurgeon often taught on how to increase in faith. One of his theme Scripture verses was, "We ought always to thank God for you, brothers, and rightly so, because your faith is growing more and more . . ." (2 Thessalonians 1:3, NIV). However, Spurgeon did not demean a person for little faith. Rather, he encouraged great faith, declaring, "Little faith will bring your souls to Heaven, but great faith will bring Heaven to your souls."[35] Like Taylor and Müller, Spurgeon believed that while faith is activated by discovering that Christ is at work within us, we also have a role to play in increasing our faith. Throughout his life Spurgeon's faith was challenged again and again, yet strengthened more and more. God increased his faith through the following principles.

### FAITH IS INCREASED BY PRAYING FOR MORE FAITH

Spurgeon found his faith weak at times, but through Christ he determined to overcome. Contrary to some who would claim that you have been given all the faith you need and thus you do not need to ask for faith, he exhorts, "Let us not rest contented with weak faith, but ask, like the apostles, to have it increased."[36] Some believe you need to pray for anything just once in faith, and to ask again is unbelief. But again Spurgeon, through his great example of faith, admonishes otherwise: "He who has true faith in his heart is praying all the day long. . . . If your faith does not make you pray, get rid of it, and God help you to begin again in true faith."[37]

### FAITH IS INCREASED THROUGH TRIALS

Spurgeon believed that faith grows by experience. Like Taylor and Müller, he understood the value of trials in strengthening our faith: "Faith untried may be true faith, but it is sure to be little faith. It is likely to remain stunted as long as it is without trials. Faith never prospers as well as when all things are against her. Tempests are her trainers, and lightnings are her illuminators. . . . Faith increases in solidity, assurance, and intensity the more it is exercised with tribulation."[38] Spurgeon suffered through physical affliction, attacks on his character and periodic depression. Yet through it all he testified, "I bear my willing witness that I owe more to the fire, and the hammer, and the file, than to anything else in my Lord's worship. I sometimes question whether I have ever learned anything except through the rod. When my schoolroom is darkest, I see most."[39]

Even though Spurgeon had a great healing ministry, he was nonetheless plagued by gout. He regarded this chronic, painful condition as discipline from the Lord, remarking with a positive attitude, "I rejoice that I have such a God as that; and that if He would chasten me a thousand times worse than this, I would still love Him; yea, though he slay me, yet will I trust Him."[40] When his wife, Susanna, was ill he wrote to his mother, "This hounding trouble has its bright side, and it abundantly sanctifies so that all is well."[41] But at the same time Spurgeon did not believe sickness was a punishment from God. Rather, he believed God could bestow blessing in the midst of sickness. When one of his critics was severely ill he wrote to him, not in judgment, but encouraging and blessing him, praying, "May your sick chamber be the very gate of heaven to your soul, the presence of the Lord filling the house with glory."[42]

### FAITH IS STRENGTHENED BY AN ATTITUDE OF JOY

Even in the midst of suffering much pain from gout throughout his life, Spurgeon himself found the joy of the Lord to be his strength. He advised out of his own experiences, "Let your conscious feebleness provoke you to seek the means of strength: and that means of strength is to be found in a pleasant medicine, sweet as it is profitable—the delicious and effectual medicine of 'the joy of the Lord.'"[43] He especially found that joy and strength by constantly repeating the promises of Scripture.

## FAITH IS INCREASED BY CONFESSING THE WORD OF GOD

Charles Spurgeon believed strongly in the power of the Word of God. Like faith and prayer, he considered the Word of God as a force or energy to activate within our lives: "We must hear Jesus speak if we expect Him to hear us speak. . . . Moreover, what is heard must remain, must live in us, and must abide in our character as a force and a power."[44] That force of truth is activated by faith through speaking and hearing the Word of God over and over:

> God the Holy Spirit will enable you to believe if you listen often and well to what you are commanded to believe. We believe many things because we have heard them so often. Do you not find that in everyday life if you hear a thing fifty times a day, you come to believe it? . . . The Holy Spirit often blesses this method of hearing the truth and uses it to work faith concerning what is to be believed. It is written, "Faith cometh by hearing" (Romans 10:17).[45]

Particularly in his times of depression Spurgeon gave this testimony of positive mental attitude and confession: "I find that if I can lay a promise under my tongue, like a sweet lozenge, and keep it in my mouth or mind all day long, I am happy enough."[46] He instructed that believers should take up the shield of faith, especially by repeating God's promises, declaring the glorious doctrines of the faith, proclaiming insights from scriptural illustrations and recounting how God has acted on our behalf in the earlier days.[47]

Sometimes people today refer to receiving a *rhema* from God (from the Greek term *rhema*, usually meaning "a spoken word"), a fresh word from God in due season. Although Spurgeon does not use the language of *rhema,* he describes the essence of receiving such a word from God:

> Often you cannot get at a difficulty so as to deal with it aright and find your way to a happy result. You pray, but have not the liberty in prayer which you desire. A definite promise is what you want. You try one and another of the inspired words, but they do not fit. You try again, and in due season a promise presents itself which seems to have been made for the occasion; it fits exactly as a well-made key fits the lock for which it was prepared. Having found the identical word of the living God you hasten to plead it at the throne of grace, saying, "Oh Lord, Thou hast promised this good thing unto Thy servant; be pleased to grant it!" The matter is ended; sorrow is turned to joy; prayer is heard.[48]

### FAITH IS INCREASED BY SOWING A SEED

Spurgeon was an early advocate of the "seed faith" concept of sowing and reaping: "Assurance is a flower that must first be planted as a bulb. Plant the bulb of faith first, and you shall eventually have the flower. The shriveled seed of a little faith springs upward, and then you have the ripe corn in the ear of full assurance of faith."[49] Similar to the contemporary slogan "Give to get to give," he declared, "Faith's way of gaining is giving. I must try this again and again; and I may expect that as much of prosperity as will be good for me will come to me as a gracious reward for a liberal course of action."[50] Spurgeon's wife had a similar saying, "Spend, and God will send."[51] Spurgeon appears to be one of the earliest leaders of faith to make the connection between giving and financial prosperity: "I have noticed that the most generous Christians have always been the most happy and almost invariably the most prosperous. I have seen the liberal giver rise to wealth of which he never dreamed. . . . It takes faith to act toward our God with an open hand."[52]

Speaking with his usual wit and humor, Spurgeon amusingly includes a condition to those who would strive for riches: "Of course, I may not be sure of growing rich. I shall be fat, but not too fat. Too great riches might make me as unwieldy as corpulent persons usually are, and cause me the dyspepsia of worldliness, and perhaps bring on a fatty degeneration of the heart."[53] Modern promoters of prosperity teaching would do well to heed Spurgeon's wise counsel.

## If You Are Weak in Faith, Be Encouraged and Hold on to Jesus

You may be saying, "But I am weak and small in faith." Spurgeon inspires us to hold on to what little faith we have: "Faith is weakness clinging to strength and becoming strong in so doing."[54] He speaks out of the experience of his own life, for this great man of faith sometimes felt weak in faith. Yet he found strength even in the midst of great bouts of depression and sickness:

> Faith exists in different persons in various degrees, according to the amount of their knowledge or growth in grace. Sometimes faith is little more than a simple *clinging* to Christ—a sense of dependence and a willingness to depend. . . . Thousands of God's people have no more faith than this. They know enough to cling to Jesus with all their heart and soul. . . . Jesus Christ is to them a strong and mighty Savior, a rock immovable and immutable. They cling to Him for dear life, and this clinging saves them.[55]

Spurgeon believed God enables believers to hang on with even the simplest faith in the midst of the deepest trials: "We can cling when we can do nothing else, and that is the very soul of faith. Always cling to what you know. . . . Cling to Jesus, for that is faith."[56]

Spurgeon does not berate a person for his lack of faith, but rather encourages:

> However feeble our faith may be, if it is real faith in Christ, we will reach heaven at last. . . . Your little faith has made you completely clean. You have as much right to the precious things of the covenant as the most advanced believers, for your right to covenant mercies lies not in your growth but in the covenant itself. . . . Am I poor in faith? Still in Jesus I am heir of all things.[57]

## Your Faith, Too, Can Grow and Overcome!

Spurgeon's words are just as relevant to a 21st-century faith walk. You may feel weak in faith and do not think you can attain the greatness of faith of a Spurgeon or Taylor or Müller. Spurgeon stirs us to realize that by God's grace we *can*. He bids us to act in the faith we have, no matter how small, and God will honor it and add to our faith all we need. It will become a powerful force to overcome all the challenges in our lives.

## THINK AND DISCUSS

1. What do you believe about the supernatural today? How does what you believe affect your exercise of faith?

2. How can you develop spiritual sensitivity to God and the things of God?
3. How can you tap into God's power forces of faith and prayer?
4. Read and discuss Spurgeon's application of Deuteronomy 28:13 and Isaiah 54:17. In what ways can these verses be applied to your life?
5. How can you increase your faith?
6. How should we respond when faith is weak?
7. Which of Spurgeon's principles is the most helpful to you? Why?

## READ MORE ABOUT IT

*Biographical*

Lewis Drummond, *Spurgeon: Prince of Preachers* (Grand Rapids: Kregel, 1992)

*Books by Spurgeon on Aspects of Faith*

Robert Hall, compiler and editor, *What the Holy Spirit Does in a Believer's Life* (Lynnwood, Wash.: Emerald Books, 1993)
Robert Hall, compiler and editor, *The Triumph of Faith in a Believer's Life* (Lynnwood, Wash.: Emerald Books, 1994)
Robert Hall, compiler and editor, *The Power of Prayer in a Believer's Life* (Lynnwood, Wash.: Emerald Books, 1993)
Robert Hall, compiler and editor, *Spiritual Warfare in a Believer's Life* (Lynnwood, Wash.: Emerald Books, 1993)

### Devotional Books by Spurgeon

*Faith's Checkbook* (Chicago: Moody Press, n.d.)

*Morning by Morning* (Old Tappan, N.J.: Fleming H. Revell, 1984)

*1000 Devotional Thoughts* (Grand Rapids: Baker Book House, 1976)

# 4

## Phoebe Palmer
### (1807–1874)
### Trailblazing Woman of Faith

---

**Faith principle:**

*Faith comes by full surrender and trust.*

---

Phoebe Worrall Palmer rejoiced in her new son, Alexander, born on her first wedding anniversary. But tragically, at the age of eleven months he died. She grieved deeply, claiming that the Lord had taken him from her: "I felt that he was *taken* away—not *given* up—*torn* from my embrace, not a *free-will offering.*"

The following spring she gave birth to another son whom she named Samuel. She gave all her attention to her baby, giving up all other activities. She remarked, "Now that God has made up my loss, I will live for one dear object—I will have done with those more extended expectations, and absorb my mind's energies in this beloved one." But Samuel died just seven weeks later.

Phoebe was crushed. She sought the Lord and came to understand that she had made idols of her two children. She determined never to do so again.

Three years later she gave birth to a healthy baby girl whom she named Sarah. Two years later, however, after giving birth to another daughter, Eliza, both Phoebe and her new daughter nearly died. Lying near death, she was assured about her salvation but prayed that she wanted to live for the Lord. Both Phoebe and Eliza recovered, and she resolved to serve the Lord more fully.

Not long after, she left her baby in the care of a nurse-maid. The nurse accidentally knocked an alcohol lamp into the baby's crib, and Eliza was burned to death. In agony, Phoebe wept before the Lord. Opening her Bible, she came upon the words "O the depth of the riches both of the wisdom and knowledge of God! How unsearchable are his judgments, and his ways are past finding out!" (Romans 11:33, KJV). In the midst of her intense sorrow she heard the Holy Spirit whispering to her. She sensed God saying not to look at "second causes," whether due to her nurse or herself or Satan, but to trust that God had allowed this trial for a good and holy purpose.

From then on she "made a conscious choice to trust God's goodness and love." "From that hour," she reflected, "as a weaned child, I rested down and kissed the rod"—she was accepting the chastening of the Lord. This event became a turning point in her faith and walk with God, for "she thought of the day of Eliza's death as the beginning of her concern for evangelism."[1]

Through these apparent tragedies she saw the hand of God, which causes all things to work together for good. Her key to finding the faith, not only to carry on in the midst of sorrow but to live victoriously over such painful experiences, came through full surrender to God and total trust in Him. In the words of an old hymn, "Trust and obey, for there's no other way to be happy in Jesus, but to trust and obey."

## Meet Phoebe Palmer

Phoebe Palmer, another contemporary of George Müller and evangelist Charles Finney, became a popular Methodist holiness leader in the mid-1800s. She wrote extensively on faith, especially in a collection of writings, first published in 1848, entitled *Faith and its Effects*. Her teachings on faith were developed from eighteenth-century Methodist leaders.

Phoebe Palmer is regarded by many scholars and Christian leaders as one of the most influential Christian women of the nineteenth century. The great preacher of the Brooklyn Tabernacle, T. DeWitt Talmage, praised her as the "Columbus of the Higher Life," remarking that she "showed to the Church of God that there were mountain peaks of Christian satisfaction that it had never attained."[2] She and her husband, Walter, became catalysts for revival in many places, and she was dubbed a "female Charles Finney."[3]

It has been estimated that more than 25,000 people came to Christ through her ministry. She not only promoted and expanded the acceptability of the ministry of laity and women but also had an impact upon significant Christian leaders. Christian leaders influenced by Palmer included the following:

- *Thomas Upham*, professor of philosophy and early psychologist
- *B. T. Roberts*, founder of the Free Methodist Church
- *Hannah Whitall Smith*, author of the classic *The Christian's Secret of a Happy Life*

- *A. B. Simpson*, founder of The Christian and Missionary Alliance (C&MA)
- Methodist social activist *Frances Willard*
- Episcopalian medical doctor and faith healing leader *Charles Cullis*
- evangelist *Dwight L. Moody*, who followed her revival practices[4]

Phoebe Palmer expressed that God intends the life we live to be a life of faith. She declared the principle that God is "immovable in faithfulness." Thus, we can implicitly and fully trust Him. His Word is authoritative and we can fully depend on His Word. In order for His Word to have an effect we must speak by faith and "declare in the strongest testimony, His faithfulness in fulfilling His promises." Then the fruits of holiness will inevitably follow.[5] We will look at seven principles of Phoebe Palmer's "life of faith."

### Faith and Holiness Are Linked

Holiness was the "burning passion" of Phoebe Palmer, both for her own personal life and for all Christians. To Phoebe, faith and holiness go hand in hand. She found that faith enables a person to be made holy, and confession of one's faith enables a person to retain holiness of life. This connection she called "sanctifying faith." She proclaimed, "Holiness is a blessing which it is now your privilege and also your duty to enjoy."[6] She believed that "holiness is power."[7] Holiness comes through a yielded life; that is, by full surrender to God and trusting Him to change and mold us, not by striving to be holy in our own efforts. She called this the baptism or filling of the Spirit. Phoebe's life models for us a heart for holiness that plays a vital role in living a Christian life of faith and power.

## Through Sanctifying Faith You Can Kindle Revival

The prayers, teaching, faith and yielded lives of Phoebe Palmer and her husband resulted in the great "laymen's revival" of 1857–1859. Through meetings Phoebe and her husband held in Canada in the summer and fall of 1857, more than two thousand people were converted. Word of the Canadian revivals and the Palmers' emphasis on lay ministry then spread to New York City. What began as noon prayer meetings for businessmen launched a nationwide revival, and from the fall of 1857 to the fall of 1858 became known as the "year of miracles."[8]

What stirred such revival? Like Spurgeon and many other evangelical leaders of their time, the Palmers believed laws "govern God's 'moral universe' just as there are laws governing the physical universe."[9] Similar to Charles Finney, they believed that "true revivals are a result of a law,"[10] which includes the law of faith. This means, first, that God "cannot work where unbelief prevails, consistently with the order of his government." They emphasized that "believing meetings," not just prayer meetings, are needed to awaken God's people and stir His Spirit.[11] Second, sanctification, the special experience of holiness or total surrender to God as well as a life of holy living, is key to revival.[12] Thus, the law of faith combined with holiness formed "sanctifying faith," which became a powerful catalyst to stimulate revival. Finally, she testified that the efforts of ordinary lay people, filled with the Spirit and walking by faith and obedience, can kindle revival. These principles had great impact, for most of the places where Phoebe and her husband ministered experienced revival power, with thousands converted and empowered with the Holy Spirit, mostly through the ministry of consecrated men and women.

## Confess Your Blessing

As a young woman, Phoebe Palmer was terrified of speaking in public. When she received her experience of sanctifying faith, she was convicted by the Lord to testify according to Romans 10:9–10, "That if you confess with your mouth, 'Jesus is Lord,' and believe in your heart that God raised him from the dead, you will be saved. For it is with your heart that you believe and are justified, and it is with your mouth that you confess and are saved" (NIV). For Phoebe, again it was an act of full surrender and trust to yield her tongue to the Lord and confess what He had done for her to hundreds, even thousands.[13] As she took the step of faith to testify, God in turn gave her boldness. Her act of faith and obedience launched this timid young woman into a public-speaking career where she ministered to thousands for more than thirty years.

From taking that step she learned the principle of confessing her faith positively. You may have thought the concept came from the modern Word of Faith movement, but, in reality, the idea is centuries old. It is found even in the writings of the early Church Fathers. Closer to our times, origins of positive faith confessions can be detected in seventeenth- and eighteenth-century Pietist leaders like August Hermann Francke (who influenced George Müller). They penned personal confessions of faith based on Scripture that are remarkably akin to modern faith confessions.[14] These Pietist leaders circulated such principles of faith confessions to the Moravians, who likewise transmitted them to the Methodist movement. One such example is Moravian missionary Peter Bohler, who encouraged John Wesley, "Preach faith until you have it, and when you have it, then preach *faith.*"

From Methodist leaders Phoebe Palmer learned and applied these faith principles and then developed them further and popularized them. Based on her experience and these verses of Scripture, she wrote letters to friends, counseling them:

> Do not forget that believing with the heart, and confessing with the mouth, stand closely connected. . . . Your heart has believed, but your lips have not fully, freely, and habitually made confession. And thus your part of the work has been left in part unfulfilled. . . . You became "cautious in professing the blessing," and have "ceased to comply with the condition" laid down by God.[15]

She further cautioned that if we "claim the blessing" but do not continue to persevere in regular testimony, we can lose the blessing.[16] Recalling her own attitudes in times of trial, she testified that by our own confessions of faith or negativism, "We pronounce our own blessings and curses."[17]

### Speak with Faith, but Don't Name and Claim It

Because of her emphasis on positive confession, some religious leaders of her day accused her of what today would be called "name it and claim it." While her teaching sounds almost strikingly similar to modern faith theology, Palmer would not endorse current teaching by some that you can "name and claim" anything you want by a formula of positive confession in Jesus' name. On the contrary, she cautioned against people who proclaimed what she called "faithism," which she defined as "telling others to 'only believe you have it, and you have got it.'"[18] Evidently, a kind of "name it and claim it" was being propagated in her day as well. For Palmer, a believer can only claim the promises of God under certain conditions, as her biographer notes: "Though faith is the 'key,' it can only open doors when it is used in its proper context of divine requirements and promises, that which forms what Palmer calls 'continuous *chain* of gospel privilege.'"[19]

She did not believe, as do some positive confession advocates today, that God wants you to be rich, and all you have to do is confess it. Such an idea would be horrifying to her as worldly, materialistic and incompatible with a life of holiness. In fact, she and her husband were quite well-to-do because of her husband's medical practice and her writing and speaking engagements, yet they were not ostentatious. Rather, Phoebe shunned fashionable dress and society parties and teas. Her social contacts were solely for spiritual purposes. Dr. and Mrs. Palmer eventually transferred their membership from a prestigious and wealthy Methodist church to a small, struggling mission work in order to avoid the "embarrassment of riches."[20]

While they sometimes did lodge in first-class cabins when traveling by ship, they did not regard them as necessary. Sometimes they left their first-class accommodations in order to fellowship with those in other lodgings, remarking that they enjoyed the company of the people in lower-class lodgings more. On one particular occasion Dr. and Mrs. Palmer held a worship service for second-class passengers. Phoebe described the experience as being in the presence of "heaven's nobility." She considered she was obeying the Word of the Lord: "Mind not high things, but condescend to men of low estate" (Romans 12:16).[21] It was her view that in order to keep a blessing from God, believers needed to shun conformity to the world, especially in matters of dress, possessions and use of time.[22]

Her experience with God at the death of her daughter Eliza had changed her attitude toward the things of the world. One of her biographers remarked:

> This newfound sense of close approach to Jesus gave her a corresponding sense of distance from the world. Things that had become important lost their significance. After being so close to Jesus, she was no longer jealous for her husband's professional preferment or her own worldly prosperity. As she explained it, "I have been weaned from the world."[23]

## Faith Engages in Spiritual Warfare

Phoebe Palmer perceived the reality of spiritual warfare and recognized that the Christian has both the right and responsibility by faith to do battle with the spiritual forces of darkness. Soon after her experience of sanctifying faith, or baptism in the Spirit, she had a vivid dream of a demon entering their house. She woke up with a scream and, in that instant, began to doubt her experience of sanctification. "If God had really given her this blessing," she pondered, "why did she now seem more open to Satan's influence than before?"[24] Though she did not have an answer at that moment, she sensed the peace of God and went back to sleep.

Within two hours she experienced another dream in which an angel appeared to her. Suspicious of its origin because of the earlier dream, she nonetheless received an assurance from God. Her husband returned home from a house call in the middle of the night, discovering her kneeling and praising God for the victory over the demonic temptation. For a period of about two weeks she continued to have periodic "assaults of satanic doubt" so that, she expressed, "My whole frame was in feverish excitement." The light of victory broke through when she realized that laying herself on the altar as a living (continual) sacrifice, according to Romans 12:1, meant that Jesus was continually cleansing her from all unrighteousness. Her doubts vanished, and the satanic accusations ceased. The Spirit of God had enlightened her reason, and her new understanding of the truth of God's Word had set her free.[25]

Palmer had a sense that spiritual warfare was a vital part of the work of the ministry. She had a high regard for pastors and ministers of the Gospel and gave them her full support, calling them "ambassadors of the King of kings." She viewed the pastor as a "captain of Israel," who was expected to lead his congregation in "the arts of holy warfare" and assault Satan's strongholds.[26]

She did not relegate the task of spiritual warfare to the clergy alone, however, for she understood the authority and power of every believer to be involved in lay ministry. Fond of writing poetry, she penned these verses on spiritual warfare:

> Christians, to arms! Behold in sight
> The treacherous, threatening sons of night!
> To arms! Or thou are put to flight,
>     Attest thy glorious chivalry.
> Armor thou hast. O! haste to use
> Ere thou the skill to use it lose!
> Powerless thou art if thou refuse
>     To arm thee with this panoply.
> Rise! Clothed in strength, assert thy right!
> Thou of the first-born sons of light—
>     Christ is thy strength, and in his might
>     Go forth, and his salvation see.[27]

Although the full understanding of the authority of the believer would not be taught until many decades later (see chapter 11 in this book on John MacMillan), Phoebe Palmer had begun to call Christians in faith to exercise their right to overcome the "sons of night."

## Faith Operates with Controlled Emotionalism

Holiness meetings of the 1800s in the Methodist, Keswick and Higher Life movements were sometimes quite emotional, not unlike later Pentecostal meetings, replete with people weeping, laughing, shouting, singing boisterously, trembling and falling under the power of the Holy Spirit. Although such emotional demonstrations sometimes accompanied the Palmers' meetings, they encouraged seeking the Lord for sanctification "irrespective of emotion or sensible demonstration."[28] In other words, emotional outbursts could be viewed as genuinely accompanying a work of the Holy Spirit and were often accepted as such, yet were neither encouraged nor sought. When things got too wild, Phoebe Palmer would pull in the reins and tone down the meetings to avoid "extravagancies, and disorderly fanatical demonstrations."[29] One reporter commented:

> She could manage a large meeting with perfect ease, and wonderful effect. In the midst of excitement, while many of her sex were wild with transport, her complete self-possession and poise were wonderful. When the tendency was to extravagance and violent demonstration she could check the tornado, and do it almost insensibly to the congregation.[30]

The example of Phoebe Palmer and other Holiness leaders shows us today that, on one hand, we do not have to be afraid of expressing emotion, nor, on the other hand, do we have to be overly demonstrative.

## Faith Is the Evidence, Not External Manifestations

Accordingly, Palmer viewed emotion and feelings as effects of the working of the Holy Spirit, but not as necessary evidence. While some in her day were expecting the experience of sanctification or baptism with the Spirit to be proven by some emotional experience or physical manifestation, Phoebe insisted that faith alone in the Word of God is the evidence (see Hebrews 11:1).[31] She believed it is "naked faith in a naked promise." Palmer popularized the idea of the "second blessing" or "baptism in the Holy Spirit," taught by earlier Methodist leaders. Her teaching would lay the foundation for the roots of Pentecostalism, but she would disagree strongly with the Pentecostal teaching that a certain gift or manifestation is the evidence of the filling of the Spirit. Later evangelist F. F. Bosworth, who circulated in evangelical and Pentecostal circles (and himself prayed in tongues), advocated her position, declaring that faith is the evidence of the Spirit's empowering, not speaking in tongues.

Phoebe Palmer teaches us today that though God may sometimes grant signs of His presence and power, we do not have to (indeed, we should not) look for signs and wonders. She teaches us that, at its very root, faith involves full surrender and implicit trust in God. She shows us, along with other great evangelical leaders like Charles Spurgeon and A. B. Simpson, the validity and power of positive confession of our faith, yet avoids the excesses and errors of "name it and claim it" theology.

## You, Too, Can Have Full Surrender and Trust!

Do you want to have the great faith of Phoebe Palmer? Fully surrender yourself to God, and trust Him wholly.

Have a passion for holiness. Confess the blessings God desires to impart to you. Exercise the authority God has given you to overcome the forces of the evil one. Be not afraid of emotion, but neither get caught up in it. Do not look for physical evidence or manifestations, but look to Jesus. Then you will walk in fullness of faith.

## THINK AND DISCUSS

1. What do you need to surrender to God fully so you can completely trust Him?
2. How do faith and holiness work together? How are faith and holiness combined in your life? Is there some dimension of holiness you need in order to exercise faith?
3. How do faith and holiness stir revival? How can you stir revival in your church and community?
4. In what ways is it appropriate to make positive confessions of our blessings? In what ways is it improper to "name and claim" blessings from God?
6. Describe how spiritual warfare is taking place in your life. How can you gain the victory?
7. Do you consider yourself an emotional or an unemotional person? If you are emotional, do you need to learn to control your emotions in some areas? If you are unemotional, do you need to become free to express emotion at times? When is it appropriate to be emotional?
8. What are the dangers of seeking manifestations? Can a person desire God to work supernaturally without seeking inappropriately?
9. Which of Phoebe Palmer's principles of faith is the most helpful to you? Why?

## READ MORE ABOUT IT

### Biographical

Harold E. Raser, *Phoebe Palmer: Her Life and Thought* (Lewiston, N.Y.: Edwin Mellen Press, 1987)
Charles Edward White, *The Beauty of Holiness* (Grand Rapids: Francis Asbury Press, 1986)

### Book by Phoebe Palmer

*The Devotional Writings of Phoebe Palmer* (New York: Garland Press, 1985)

# 5

## Hannah Whitall Smith
(1832–1911)

*Advocate of Higher Life Faith*

---

**Faith principle:**

*Faith is the Christian's secret of a happy life.*

---

In 1875, after a series of fiery trials, Hannah Whitall Smith and her husband, Robert Pearsall Smith, were at the height of their ministry. Robert had experienced two nervous breakdowns a few years earlier, but he seemed to have recovered and had become an internationally acclaimed evangelist. Hannah had struggled through her husband's illnesses as well as the deaths of three of her children, but she had emerged victorious to publish her classic and popular book *The Christian's Secret of a Happy Life.*

Robert had just completed a highly successful series of evangelistic campaigns in Europe. Hannah joined him in Brighton, England, along with Presbyterian Higher Life leader William Boardman and others, to found a series of deeper life meetings in what would become known as the Keswick Holiness movement. In the midst of their flourishing ministry, the principles of Hannah's secret to a happy Christian life would be tried even more severely.

While the Brighton conferences were continuing, one young woman whom Robert had counseled was in deep distress and pled with him to come to her room to pray for her. Although he was much older and claimed only a fatherly concern for her, she reported he had attempted to seduce her. The other leaders of the conference believed her and abruptly canceled all of Robert's meetings. The local newspaper reported it as an exposé with the headline "Famous Evangelist Found in Bedroom of Adoring Female Follower." Robert's preaching career in Europe was instantly shattered and he suffered another nervous breakdown.[1]

Though Hannah bemoaned her husband's lack of discretion, she believed he was innocent. In the midst of this trial she wrote, "But the Lord has taught us the lesson of living moment by moment and I am not anxious."[2] They ceased all public life and ministry and returned to their home in Philadelphia in disgrace. Hannah contented herself with caring for her mentally distraught husband, her children and her dying father.

About a year later some supporters and minister friends urged them to overcome the scandals and start fresh again in the United States. So they began a series of meetings in which Robert's "old touch" (anointing from the Lord) seemed to have returned and the former presence of the Lord was evident to everyone. Robert, however, felt none of the enthusiasm Hannah and the others were experiencing, and his faith was gradually slipping away from him. Hannah struggled with why and how God could have allowed all this to happen.[3] She began to have her own doubts, at one point writing to a friend, "I remain an old dry stick."[4] Yet ultimately she did not waver in her faith.

By 1882, still grieving from the death of yet another daughter in 1880, she discovered that Robert was engaging in an affair. She remained married to him, but they went their own ways for the most part. Yet this was not the end of the tragedies. Her three grown children, influenced by their father's loss of faith, one by one fell prey to the intellectual skepticism taking hold in their day. One of her daughters even married the famed atheist Bertrand Russell. Two of her children also appeared to inherit their father's emotional and mental instability, probably what we would describe today as a bipolar (manic-depressive) disorder.

## Meet Hannah Whitall Smith

Although Hannah naturally suffered through periods of deep grief and depression, she maintained a buoyancy that enabled her to emerge victoriously. She continued to minister and to write and became involved in the temperance and women's right to vote movements. She believed in and modeled the faithfulness of God. In the midst of the trials of her later years she wrote of her faith:

God alone is unchangeable. What we call "spiritual blessings" are full of the element of change. The prayer which is answered today may seem to be unanswered tomorrow. The promises, once so gloriously fulfilled, may cease to have any apparent fulfillment. The spiritual blessing which was at one time such a joy may be utterly lost. Nothing of all we once trusted in and rested in may be left us but the hungry and longing memory of it all. But when all else is gone, God is still left. Nothing changes Him. He is the same, yesterday, today and forever, and in Him is neither variableness, nor shadow caused by turning. And the soul that finds its joy in Him alone can suffer no wavering.[5]

It was such faith that enabled her to overcome the trials and tragedies of her life. She declared, "Faith is the conquering law of the universe,"[6] and maintained that the Christian's secret of a happy life was a "life of faith," of abiding in Christ. She did not define happiness in the usual popular sense but as "inward rest and outward victory."[7] Even though her life and family seemed to be in turmoil all around her, she was able to find personal victory and inner peace for herself. What, then, were the keys that sustained her faith and maintained "the Christian's secret of a happy life"?

## Detach from the World and Abandon Self

Having been raised in a Quaker background, Hannah learned from the old evangelical mystics like Fénelon and Madame Guyon to become detached from the world and to abandon her own self for the sake of God. This, ironically, is the first key to biblical happiness and a life of faith: losing your life in order to gain it. If we do not make the detachment ourselves, Hannah advised, God may have to do it for us. Out of her own experience she wrote that God may grant us prosperity, but then it brings spiritual detriment to our lives, so that our

> need for God is in danger of becoming far off and vague. Then the Lord is obliged to put an end to it all. Our prosperity crumbles around us like a house built on the sand. We are tempted to think He is angry with us. But in truth, it is not anger, but tenderest love. His love compels Him to take away the outward prosperity that

84

is keeping our souls from entering into the interior spiritual Kingdom of which we long to be part.[8]

Near the end of her life she reflected back over the years on what she called God's "shaking" process:

> The old Bible teachers [mystics] used to lecture on what they called *detachment*. This referred to cutting the soul loose from all that could hold it back from God. This need for detachment is the reason for many of our shakings. We cannot follow the Lord fully as long as we are tied tightly to anything else. It would be like a boat trying to sail out into the boundless ocean while it is still tied fast to the shore. . . . We must be detached from every earthly tie. . . .
>
> Those souls who abandon the self life and give themselves up to the Lord to be fully possessed by Him find that He takes possession of the inner springs of their being.[9]

Paradoxically, it is by losing ourselves and all else that we can really live a life of overcoming faith. For Hannah, it was not so much that we change our faith, but rather that our faith changes us. Thus, she delighted in asserting that faith is "a discovery, not an attainment."[10] She avowed, "You are not asked to have faith in yourself, and would be in a very wrong condition of soul if you had."[11] Faith is not something we struggle to attain, but a restful trust in God's goodness working in harmony with our obedience.

### Maintain a Steadfast Belief in the Goodness of God

This is not to say that because God "shakes" us He does not care about our material welfare. On the contrary, God *is* interested in providing for our needs. In those times of shaking, Hannah learned that God is good all the time in spite of the circumstances and that God would cause all things to work together for good. For her, though, the focus was not in getting, but trusting. Hannah explained, "This life of faith, then . . . consists in just this,—being a child in the Father's house." Giving the example of an adopted child she visited in a wealthy home, she said:

> If nothing would so grieve and wound the loving hearts around her as to see this little child beginning to be worried or anxious about herself in any way,—about whether her food and clothes would be provided, or how she was to get her education or her future support,—how much more must the great, loving heart of our God and Father be grieved and wounded at seeing His children taking so much anxious care and thought! . . . Who is the best cared for in every household? Is it not the little children?[12]

She had come to the realization that the heart of God as our Father is pure self-sacrificing goodness:

> I have discovered therefore that the statement of the fact that "God is good," is really, if we only understand it, a sufficient and entirely satisfactory assurance that our interests will be safe in His hands. Since He is good, He cannot fail to do His duty by us, and, since He is unselfish, He must necessarily consider our interests before His own. When once we are assured of this, there can be nothing left to fear. . . . The only place, therefore, of permanent and abiding peace is to be found in an acquaintance with the goodness and unselfishness of God.[13]

When we have this revelation of God, our faith becomes a solid rock in all the storms of life.

## Determine to Be Satisfied with God Alone

When a person lives in that walk (she called it a *walk*, not a *state*) of detachment or abandonment, and trusts in the inherent goodness of God, then Hannah averred, "God is enough"—nothing else is needed. A person's happiness comes not in family or friends or success, but in God alone: "Better and sweeter than health, or friends, or money, or fame, or prosperity, is the adorable will of God."[14] She explained her faith in the sufficiency of God in every situation of life:

This, then, is what I mean by God being enough. It is that we find in Him, the fact of His existence and of His character, all that we can possibly want for everything. God is, must be, our answer to every question and every cry of need. If there is any lack in the One who has undertaken to save us, nothing supplementary we can do will avail to make it up; and if there is not lack in Him, then He of Himself and in Himself is enough. . . .

The all-sufficiency of God ought to be as complete to the child of God as the all-sufficiency of a good mother is to the child of that mother. We all know the utter rest of the little child in the mother's presence and the mother's love. That its mother is there is enough to make all fears and all troubles disappear. The child does not need the mother to make any promises; she herself, just as she is, without promises and without explanations, is all that the child needs. . . .

God's saints in all ages have known this and have realized that God was enough for them. Job said out of the depths of sorrow and trials, which few can equal, "Though he slay me, yet will I trust in Him." . . .

Therefore, O doubting and sorrowful heart, cannot thee realize with Job and the saints of all ages that nothing else is needed to quiet all thy fears, but just this—that God is.

God is enough! God is enough for time. God is enough
for eternity. God is enough![15]

This truth became a serendipity to her and she testified:

All the old familiar texts—they were literally illuminated
with a new meaning. Every page of the Bible seemed to
declare in trumpet tones the reality of a victorious and
triumphant life to be lived by faith in the Lord Jesus
Christ. My whole soul was afire with my discovery. . . .
I saw that He was not only my Savior for the future, but
He was also my all-sufficient Savior for the present. He
was my Captain to fight my battles for me, in order that
I need not fight them myself; He was my Burden-bearer
to carry my burdens, in order that I might roll them
off of my own weak shoulders; He was my Fortress to
hide me from my enemies; my Shield to protect me;
my Guide to lead me; my Comforter to console me; my
Shepherd to care for me. No longer did I need to care
for, and protect, and fight for myself. It was all in the
hands of One who was mighty to save; and what could
I do but trust Him?[16]

## Avoid Negative Thoughts and Conversation

In 1877, when her own faith was being weakened by
her husband's complaints about his troubles and doubts,
Hannah wrote to Robert in her quaint Quaker language,
"I want thee to promise not to whisper a word of thy
perplexities into my ears. It is a ticklish seat on top of
a greased pole."[17] She felt her own faith was precarious
and wanted to avoid any pessimistic thinking that might
cause her faith to fail.

She had written just two years earlier, "It is an inexorable rule in the spiritual life that according to our faith
it is to be unto us; and of course this rule must work both
ways, and therefore we may fairly expect that it will be

also unto us according to our doubts."[18] She recognized that her husband was reaping the consequences of his own negativism.

Conversely, she maintained the importance of surrounding oneself with strong, faith-filled Christians. She had written in *The Christian's Secret of a Happy Life,* "How is it possible to live by faith if human agencies, in which it would be wrong and foolish to trust, are to have a prevailing influence in molding our lives?"[19] To Robert she wrote, "I think it is a very critical time with thee, and if thee wants to get back to the old place, thee must put thyself under the right sort of influences."[20] She stressed the importance of "speaking right" and avoiding "bad reports," which could become contagious.[21] She observed from her husband's behavior the phenomenon of self-fulfilling prophecy through his pessimism and doubts.

She did not insist, however, as some do today that just mentioning a negative fact such as "I am sick" is a negative confession and would cause negative consequences. It is also important to note that she did not consider sickness necessarily due to a lack of faith or sin. Once when she was suffering from chronic diarrhea, insomnia and trembling, some of her religious friends suggested that if she was really strong in her faith she would not be ill. She responded by writing, "It seems to me a dreadful thing to make all the poor suffering invalids feel that they are yielding to the power of the devil in being sick, and that every pain they have is a sin."[22]

### Assert What God Says Regardless of Feeling

Not only did Hannah stress avoiding negative thoughts and conversation, but also making positive assertions of faith. "Faith is simply to believe and assert the thing that God says . . . whatever the circumstances are."[23] These are principles of faith confession similar to those of Phoebe Palmer. She advocated, "Put your will, then, over on the believing side. Say, 'Lord, I will believe, I do believe,' and continue to say it."[24] Speaking out of her trials with her husband and children, she counseled, "You must meet all assaults of doubt and discouragement with the simple assertion that you are in the fortress [referring to Psalm 91:1–2]. . . . You must declare that other people do as they may, you are going to abide in your divine dwelling place forever."[25] She suggested repeating a Scripture over and over, each time emphasizing a different word.[26] After the deaths of three of her children and her husband's two nervous breakdowns, Hannah testified:

> I have begun to assert over and over, my faith in Him, in the simple words, "God is my Father; I am His forgiven child; He does love me; Jesus saves me; Jesus saves me now!" The victory has always been complete. . . . Let your unchanging declaration be from henceforth, "Though He slay me, yet will I trust in Him." When doubts come, meet them, not with arguments, but with assertions of faith. . . . Go at once and confess your faith, in the strongest language possible, somewhere or to someone. If you cannot do this by word of mouth, write it in a letter, or repeat it over and over in your heart to the Lord.[27]

While strongly advocating repeated declarations of our faith, Hannah nevertheless also gave a warning to those who would try to make an incantation or magical formula out of positive confession: "But we must not say it with our lips only, and then by our actions deny our words. We must say it with our whole being, with thought, word, and action."[28] It is then an attitude of heart and soul, not of words only: "Let us settle it then, that the language of our souls must be, from now on, not the *much less* of unbelief, but the *much more* of faith. . . . Our failure comes because we have substituted our *much less* for God's *much more.*"[29]

## Operate by the Law of Faith

Hannah thus understood this principle to operate as the "law of faith": "It is an inexorable rule in the spiritual life that according to our faith it is to be unto us. . . ."[30] For her, faith was "the law of creation."[31] Romans 4:17 is a favorite verse among some modern faith teachers. Hannah Whitall Smith appears to be one of the earliest to make reference to this Scripture: "Faith, we are told, 'calleth those things which be not as though they were.' Calling them brings them into being."[32] This is not man creating things out of nothing, as some today teach, but God creatively working as we speak the promises of His Word. She also likens the law of faith to the law of gravitation, or as a magnetic pull.[33] As we operate in the faith we have, it attracts like faith, and faith is increased.

## Test Impressions, Feelings and Personal Applications of the Promises of God

As a Quaker, Hannah adhered to the typical Quaker practice of listening for the inner voice of God. However, she cautioned against trusting the inner voice rather than Scripture and stressed the need for discernment: "If we fail to search out and obey the Scripture rule, where there is one, and look instead for an inward voice, we shall open ourselves to delusions, and shall almost inevitably get into error."[34] She recognized that God does sometimes lead through impressions, but those impressions must be in harmony with the Scripture, providential circumstances and the conviction of our own higher judgment. She warned, "We must never forget that 'impressions' can come from other sources as well as the Holy Spirit." They can come from strong personalities around us, from our physical conditions or from spiritual enemies. "It is not enough to have a leading," she cautioned, "we must find out the source of that leading before we give ourselves up to follow it."[35] There are times when human sense and emotion are contrary to faith, so faith must come before feeling.[36]

Ironically, at the very time her book was released, her husband did not abide by her counsel but was involved with a "secret doctrine" being taught in some Holiness circles in which it was believed the Holy Spirit sends thrills up and down the body.[37] Her words forewarning the danger of deception became tragically prophetic of her own husband.

### Recognize You Are in a Struggle between Good and Evil

Although she attributed most human problems to the life of self and the flesh, she also recognized that a spiritual battle is often involved in our trials. When her daughter Mary was about to marry someone outside the faith, she recalled and took heed to the words written to her by a friend: "There is a dreadful struggle going on in that family between the powers of good and evil."[38] She was aware that the spirit of unbelief infiltrating the Church was causing disillusionment and deception to her family as well.

When her husband died she regarded his death as a release from the delusions of darkness. She wrote to a friend of "the strong sense I have had ever since my dear husband was permitted to escape from the earthly tabernacle, that his long time of darkness is over and that God's light has shown upon him at last."[39] She attributed his mental and emotional condition to both spiritual and physical causes: "I have always felt sure his clouded spiritual life was the result of physical causes and I believe it was truly the 'binding of Satan' from which deliverance has come."[40] Years before the condition manic-depression was discovered frequently to involve chemical imbalance, Hannah discerned that Robert had a physical problem aggravated and worsened by spiritual forces of darkness causing delusions in his mind. To her mind, healing and release from spiritual, emotional and physical bondage for Robert came through his death.

Hannah's biographer, Marie Henry, sums up her life of faith:

> Hannah Whitall Smith's resiliency would surprise people all of her life. Knocked down, time after time, hounded by doubts and confusion, she had a gift for dealing with defeat and rebounding from despair. There was a prevailing buoyancy in her soul, an aliveness and sense of adventure in her spirit.
>
> Hannah would have said very simply that her constantly deepening faith kept her from losing her enthusiasm for life, that it was her steadfast belief in the goodness of God that lightened her spirits and enabled her to maintain her vitality.[41]

## You, Too, Can Find the Secret of a Happy Life of Faith!

Through these principles, you, too, can walk such a life of faith in the midst of trials and tragedies, loss and grief, and find the Christian's secret of a happy life. Second Corinthians 4:7–9 capsulizes the experience of Hannah Whitall Smith: "But we have this treasure in earthen vessels, so that the surpassing greatness of the power will be of God and not from ourselves; we are afflicted in every way, but not crushed; perplexed, but not despairing; persecuted, but not forsaken; struck down, but not destroyed" (NASB).

Like Hannah, by trusting in the goodness of God, becoming detached from the world and finding satisfaction in God alone, you can have a peace that passes human understanding. By avoiding negativism and making positive confessions of the Word of God and recognizing the reality of spiritual conflict, you can exercise the law of faith, walk in confidence and overcome the problems of your life.

## THINK AND DISCUSS

1. In what ways are you attached to the world and self? How does that affect your walk of faith?
2. How can you see the goodness of God in the midst of trial? Describe a time when you experienced God's goodness in trial.
3. Explain the all-sufficiency of God. In what ways can God be enough for you?
4. What negative thoughts or influences are affecting your life? How can you deal with them?
5. What are you struggling with in your life now? What Scripture verses or promises of God can you assert and repeat to give you encouragement and strengthen your faith?
6. How do you know if your impressions and feelings are from God? When might they not be of God?
7. Which of Hannah Smith's principles of faith is the most helpful to you? Why?

## READ MORE ABOUT IT

### Biographical

Marie Henry, *Hannah Whitall Smith* (Minneapolis: Bethany House Publishers, 1984)

### Books by Hannah Whitall Smith

*The Christian's Secret of a Happy Life* (Old Tappan, N.J.: Fleming H. Revell, 1942)

*The God of All Comfort* (New Kensington, Pa.: Whitaker House, 1984)

*Living Confidently in God's Love* (New Kensington, Pa.: Whitaker House, 1984)

*The Unselfishness of God* (Princeton: Littlebrook Publishing, 1987)

# 6

# E. M. Bounds
## (1835–1913)

## God's Prayer Warrior

---

**Faith principle:**

*Unleash faith-filled prayer,
your most powerful force.*

---

Edward McKendree Bounds had become a lawyer at the age of 19, but in 1859 at the age of 24 he suddenly experienced a "second blessing" empowering of the Holy Spirit and sensed a call from God to the ministry. Shortly after this he shut down his law practice abruptly and began an intense study of the Scriptures, John Wesley's sermons, and biographies of David Brainerd and John Fletcher. He began preaching and evangelizing, becoming licensed to preach in the Methodist Church in February 1860. A year later he accepted the call to pastor a church in his home state of Missouri with the Methodist Episcopal Church, South.

Missouri had been a border state in the growing conflict over slavery, and even though E. M. Bounds' parents "had hired a slave woman as a household servant, they were neither partisan defenders of slavery nor secessionist in sentiment."[1] Sharing that position, E. M. Bounds himself tried to maintain neutrality with his new congregation, while his older brothers later joined the Union Army. A few months after Bounds became a pastor, federal troops entered Missouri. As his biographer describes it, "Bounds, while uncomfortable supporting slavery, found himself the pastor of a church that was, as people in his county saw it, invaded by hostile forces."[2] Union troops accused him of being "disloyal to the Union because of his denominational affiliation," and he was arrested, treated harshly and incarcerated in a federal prison at St. Louis with "a collection of criminals, rebel soldiers, and Confederate sympathizers. Immediately, he began ministering to scores of angry and defeated souls. He was a *de facto* Confederate chaplain even though he had neither volunteered nor signed a loyalty oath in support of the Confederate States of America."[3]

After a year and a half in prison he was released but exiled to the South, being forbidden to return to Missouri. Thus banished from the Union, he served the South as a military chaplain in Tennessee, caring deeply for the soldiers through preaching, worship, encouraging and praying for them, and staying with them even on the front lines of battle. After a great slaughter Bounds and the remaining survivors were captured. The war was soon over, and Bounds was released. He returned to Missouri briefly to visit his family, but his heart was in ministering to the defeated peoples of Tennessee. For the rest of his life he carried in his wallet the names of the Missourian soldiers he buried at Franklin, Tennessee.

## Meet E. M. Bounds

E. M. Bounds' biographer describes his attitude throughout all the injustice, disappointment, tragedy and suffering:

> The former chaplain never criticized his captors or other Yankees and northern sympathizers. . . . He never vilified the Yankees, and he was never overheard to vindicate or defend his own actions or stand. . . . As Alexander Maclaren said a century ago, "If a man considers himself to be an iron pillar, he is of no use to God. God works through broken reeds." Between 1861 and 1865 Bounds became a broken reed. God allowed him to suffer humiliation, total loss of freedom and possessions, and He made him a pilgrim. . . . He was stripped of his personal property and citizenship. . . . The five-foot-five-inch preacher with fiery eyes never complained of his lot.[4]

Bounds had learned to pray and to trust God during his Civil War days. He seldom talked about his own prayer experiences, but on a rare occasion, using the editorial "we," wrote of his personal struggle in prayer:

> In agony of soul we have sought refuge from the oppression of the world in the anteroom of heaven; the waves of despair seemed to threaten destruction, and as no way of escape was visible, we fell back, like the disciples of old, upon the power of our Lord, crying to Him to save us lest we perish. And then, in the twinkling of an eye, the thing was done. The billows sank into a calm; the howling wind died down at the divine command; the agony of soul passed into a restful peace as over the whole being there crept the consciousness of the divine presence, bringing with it the assurance of answered prayer and sweet deliverance.[5]

99

As a result of his military experience, he viewed prayer and faith in terms of spiritual warfare, declaring, "Prayer is our most formidable weapon, but the one in which we are the least skilled, the most adverse to its use."[6] He speaks of the "spiritual forces of prayer," "wrestling in prayer," "courageous faith" and "commanding faith."[7] Prayer is "the faithful sentinel," "commanding force," "holds the citadel for God" and advances the kingdom of God.[8] He took no political sides but became a prayer warrior for the Kingdom of God. Bounds went on to other pastorates and ministries to be greatly used by God:

- He became known in his lifetime for his powerful evangelistic ministry, revivals and his inspiring editorial writings. Still, most of his writings on prayer were not known then but were published after his death.

- He has become world-renowned as the "man of prayer." As the foundation of all his work was prayer, he rose at 4:00 A.M. to spend hours with God. Typically, his family would rise with him for a time of prayer and singing praises. On one occasion his daughters had some other young girls over for a slumber party, and they stayed up talking late into the night. Even so, Bounds roused them at 4:00 A.M. for prayer and praise. One of his grandchildren remarked that his "success that day was similar to the success Jesus experienced at Gethsemane. Everyone else fell asleep while the one who convened the meeting prayed on."[9]

- His writings have had great impact upon thousands, including evangelist Billy Sunday, the former baseball player.

Let us look at the principles of Bounds' faith and prayer that turned a misunderstood, mistreated and rejected preacher into a mighty warrior for God.

## Energize Your Faith through Prayer

For E. M. Bounds faith and prayer go hand in hand—two sides of the same coin. He believed, "Prayer is but the expression of faith."[10] True prayer, then, is an operation of faith; genuine prayer is praying with faith. There is no real prayer without faith and no real faith without prayer. In fact, "The life of faith perfects the prayer of faith," Bounds wrote.[11] Prayer without faith Bounds called "prayerless praying," commenting that "desire burdens the chariot of prayer, and faith drives its wheels."[12] This combination of faith and prayer, Bounds wrote, is the "energy of prayer."[13]

Faith is not only expressed through prayer, but prayer actually energizes and activates faith, taking it to new heights:

Apostolic praying was as taxing, toilsome, and imperative as apostolic preaching. They prayed mightily day and night to bring their people to the regions of faith and holiness. . . . How can a man preach who does not get his message fresh from God in the closet? How can he preach without having his faith quickened, his vision cleared, and his heart warmed by his closeting with God?[14]

Contrary to some who claim faith works without prayer, Bounds quoted Martin Luther, "If I should neglect prayer but a single day, I should lose a great deal of the fire of faith."[15]

Strong faith, Bounds asserted, comes from spending much time with God: "Hurried devotions make weak faith, feeble convictions, questionable piety. To be little with God is to be little for God. . . . It takes good time for the full flow of God into the spirit. Short devotions cut the pipe of God's full flow. It takes time in the secret places to get the full revelation of God."[16] Bounds demonstrated a living example of what he proclaimed, for he spent three to four hours daily in prayer. Some today believe a person does not need to pray much, just praise the Lord continually. This was not the attitude of this man of God. He spent hours on his back or on his face or knees before the Lord, weeping and crying out for the lost, for revival and for believers, especially preachers, to become sanctified. Many were intimidated by his life of prayer. In 46 years of ministry, no ministers and only one layman ever approached him about being mentored in the life of prayer and faith. His biographer comments, "In the last analysis few wanted to be tutored by a man who pressed them to join a life of early morning prayer, humble service, and purposeful austerity."[17] We do not need to be discouraged that we cannot attain his level of prayer. Rather we can be encouraged from his example that our faith can be energized by prayer, as was Bounds, continuing his early morning prayer habit until just months before he died at the age of 76.

### United Believing Prayer Is a Mighty Force

Earlier I mentioned that Spurgeon had preached about faith and prayer as powerful forces like electricity. Bounds also combined faith and prayer (believing prayer or prayer in faith) and declaring them together to be a mighty force. "Prayer puts God in full force in the world. . . . Prayer is not a negation. It is a positive force. . . . Prayer puts God in the matter with commanding force."[18] Bounds describes this mighty force of faith and prayer, especially as joined together with the faith and prayer of others: "The concentration and aggregation of faith, desire, and prayer increased the volume of spiritual force until it became overwhelming and irresistible in its power. Units of prayer combined, like droplets of water, make an ocean which defies resistance."[19]

For nearly three years after the Civil War Bounds ministered as a pastor to the people of the war-torn town of Franklin, Tennessee, where the great slaughter had taken place. The people of the church had become disheartened, and were full of bitterness and hatred. Every Tuesday night Bounds gathered together about six men who "really believed in the power of prayer" to pray for revival. One young man described what resulted: "God finally answered by fire. The revival just came down without any previous announcement or plan, and without the pastor sending for an evangelist to help him." Nearly 150 people "were gloriously converted."[20] This demonstrates the powerful force of faith and prayer in which Bounds believed.

It is important to understand that Bounds did not believe faith to be some kind of impersonal force or deistic law, but rather the action of God Himself. Bounds writes that "the driving power, the conquering force in God's cause is God Himself."[21] This does not mean that God is an impersonal force, but rather that faith and prayer are an expression of His divine attribute of omnipotence, His almighty power.

### Prayer-Force Produces the Anointing of the Holy Spirit

Bounds declares, "It is prayer-force that makes saints. Holy characters are formed by the power of real praying."[22] Such praying results in "unction," what we call today the anointing of the Holy Spirit. Such unction or anointing itself becomes what Bounds calls "consecration force." Bounds explains that "this divine and heavenly oil put on it by the imposition of God's hand must soften and lubricate the whole man—heart, head, spirit—until it separates him with a mighty separation from all earthly, secular, worldly, selfish motives and aims, separating him to everything that is pure and Godlike."[23] There is much talk about the anointing of God today, but such emphasis often misses Bounds' notion of "consecration force." Anointing to Bounds is not chiefly intended to be the power to perform signs and wonders, but power to stir conviction and lead people to repentance and holiness.[24] This indeed was the anointing Bounds himself possessed.

Do you want that anointing of the Holy Spirit in your life? To obtain and retain that anointing, Bounds counseled, "This unction is not an unalienable gift. It is a conditional gift, and its presence is perpetuated and increased by the same process by which it was at first secured: by unceasing prayer to God, by impassioned desires after God, by estimating it, by seeking it with tireless ardor, by deeming all else loss and failure without it."[25]

### Fervency and Persistency of Prayer Are Necessary for Victorious Faith

Some today teach that you only need to pray once, and then claim by faith. This was not the belief and practice of this prayer warrior. While he recognized God may give faith to claim a promise without further prayer, his emphasis was on the need for what the King James Version of the Bible calls "importunate prayer," praying with fervency and persistency until the answer comes. Without these, according to Bounds, our petitions are "forceless prayers."[26]

He defined importunate prayer as "a mighty movement of the soul toward God. It is a stirring of the deepest forces of the soul, toward the throne of heavenly grace. It is the ability to hold on, press on, and wait."[27] Such faith-praying needs an "array of sanctified energies bent on reaching and grappling with God, to draw from Him the treasures of His Grace."[28] One biblical scholar, who has studied the Jewish roots of the New Testament, has similarly described such action of faith as *chutzpah*, which he defines as the act of "persever[ing] with unyielding tenacity."[29] It is the struggle of Jacob with the angel of the Lord, holding onto the angel, as Jacob declared, "I will not let you go unless you bless me" (Genesis 32:26, NIV). This characterized E. M. Bounds' life of faith and prayer.

## Take Courage in Delays, Denials and Failures

Such tenacious faith is necessary to overcome the delays, unanswered prayers and seeming failures of faith. One might think that such a great man of faith and prayer would always have his prayers answered, but the truth is that E. M. Bounds suffered heavy trials. Though he believed in healing and the protection of God, two of his children and his first wife died within a five-year period. He grieved deeply, saying, "The blow is heavy on me, my heart seems literally broken. . . . I rejoice in the will of God, its wisdom and love but my heart is broken by the blow [and] it seems to spend its full force on me." Eventually he was able to testify, "I am sure it is a call to me for intense effort and a deeper consecration. I will heal by God's grace."[30] And heal he did, again and again, after each painful blow.

His experiences of ministering to and burying hundreds of men on the battlefield prepared him to receive God's comfort and strength, even as he had comforted others. Years later, writing with battlefield imagery, he reflected on all these tragedies:

> We have need, too, to give thought to that mysterious fact of prayer—the certainty that there will be delays, denials, and seeming failures, in connection with its exercise. We are to prepare for these, to brook them, and cease not in our urgent praying. Like a brave soldier, who, as the conflicts grows more stern, exhibits a superior courage than in the earlier stages of the battle; so does the praying Christian, when delay and denial face him, increase his earnest asking, and ceases not until prayer prevail.[31]

Bounds never ceased to pray earnestly and trust God implicitly.

### Implicit Trust Makes Possible Mountain-Moving Faith

For Bounds, an attitude of implicit trust is the crowning point of faith: "When a Christian believer attains to faith of such magnificent proportions as these, he steps into the realm of implicit trust. He stands without a tremor on the apex of his spiritual outreaching. He has attained faith's veritable topstone which is unswerving, unalterable, unalienable trust in the power of the living God."[32]

Such faith had Bounds that on one occasion he did not have enough money in his pocket to take a train to Atlanta where he was scheduled to preach a series of revival meetings. He and his son got on board, and he remarked to the conductor, "Take us as far as this money will go." The conductor replied, "Why, I will have to drop you off in a field somewhere!" Bounds responded, "Then that will be where the Lord wants me to be." Later a man came up to Bounds and said that his fare was taken care of to Atlanta.[33]

At a later time Bounds gave up his denominational ties in order not to compromise his convictions. This meant giving up his salary, benefits, housing and future pension, even though he needed to provide for his wife and five children. His wife supported him in his decision but asked, "Now that you have left the church, how do you propose to feed all of us?" Bounds responded, "My dear, if we are in the Lord's will, the ravens will feed us if necessary."[34] This was typical of his implicit trust in the Lord, which issued out of his life of prayer. His motto was "God will manage our affairs if we will be filled with His affairs."[35]

### Exercise Commanding Faith

The ultimate in believing prayer to E. M. Bounds is what he called "commanding faith," which is a powerful weapon against Satan. In his book *Winning the Invisible War* Bounds asserts, "Prayer brings God into the situation with commanding force. 'Ask of me things to come concerning my sons,' says God, 'and concerning the work of my hand command ye me' (Isaiah 45:11)."[36] This verse, Bounds claims, is "God's *carte blanche* to prayer."[37] Some today teach that God is not in control, but you are, that God cannot act without you, that God must do your bidding, that God must bind what you bind and loose what you loose. This is *not* what Bounds is claiming, for he writes, "Faith is only omnipotent when it is on its knees, and its outstretched hands take hold of God; then it draws to the utmost of God's capacity; for only a praying faith can get God's 'all things whatsoever.'"[38] Referring to the faith expressed in the appeal of the Syrophoenician woman, Bounds explains,

"Jesus Christ surrenders Himself to the importunity of a great faith."[39]

What Bounds is teaching is that when a person is praying in the will of God and fulfills the right conditions, God will respond to that believer's commands of faith:

> Behind the praying must lie the conditions of prayer. . . .
> They are always available to the faithful and holy, but cannot exist in a frivolous, negligent, and lazy spirit. Prayer does not stand alone. It is not an isolated performance. Prayer is connected to all the duties of the Christian life. Prayer issues from a character which is made up of the elements of a vigorous and commanding faith. Prayer honors God, acknowledges His being, exalts His power, adores His providence, and secures His aid.[40]

In other words, these "all-comprehending possibilities of prayer under the promises of God," declares Bounds, are only available "to those who meet the conditions of right praying."[41] This corresponds to Charles Spurgeon's teaching:

> You are yourself a decree. . . . Our prayers are God's decrees in another shape. . . . Do not say, "How can my prayers affect the decrees of God?" They cannot, except to the degree that your prayers are decrees, and that as they come out, every prayer that is inspired of the Holy Ghost in your soul is as omnipotent and eternal as that decree which said, "Let there be light and there was light" (Gen. 1:3). . . . The ear of God shall listen, and the hand of God shall yield to your will. God bids you cry, "Thy will be done," and your will shall be done. When you can plead His promise, then your will is His will.[42]

Likewise, A. T. Pierson, Spurgeon's interim pulpit successor, proclaimed:

Faith in God so unites to God that it passes beyond the privilege of asking to the power of commanding. This language of Christ is not that of a request, however bold, but of a *fiat*. . . . And so—marvelous fact! The child of God, laying hold by faith of the Power of the Omnipotent One, issues his fiat. . . . Obey the Law of the Power and the Power obeys you. Conform to the Laws and modes of the Spirit's operations, and in the work of God's hands you may command the Spirit's Power.[43]

This does not mean that believers are "little gods," as some would claim today. What Bounds and other classic evangelical leaders are saying is that when you are walking close to God, you know the will of God with divine certainty and can speak His words with authority, and He will thus act upon His word spoken by you in commanding faith. This is not a light thing, not a privilege to be taken for granted, and not used indiscriminately or brazenly but in confident assurance, even as George Müller reminded God of the promises of His Word.

### Believing Prayer Is Not a Magic Formula

There is a dangerous tendency among some people of faith today to reduce the law and force of faith to a magical formula, or prayer spoken with faith to an impersonal manipulative force. This is not what Bounds had in mind. On the contrary, Bounds warns, "Not that prayer has in it any talismanic force, nor that it is a fetish, but that it moves God to do things that it nominates. Prayer has no magic potent charm in itself, but is only all potent because it gets the Omnipotent God to grant its request."[44] Praying in faith can never be used for selfish motives to manipulate God or others, but it is all-powerful when practiced in humble confidence in the will of God.

## You, Too, Can Become a Mighty Prayer Warrior!

In the first decade of the twentieth century E. M. Bounds wrote words equally relevant and poignant for believers of the 21st century:

> What the Church needs today is not more machinery or better, not new organizations or more and novel methods, but men whom the Holy Ghost can use—men of prayer, men mighty in power! The Holy Ghost does not flow through methods, but through men. He does not come on machinery, but on men. He does not anoint plans, but men—men of prayer.[45]

Be a man or a woman of believing prayer, and God will use you mightily!

### Think and Discuss

1. Explain the relationship between prayer and faith and how they work together.
2. In what way is prayer a force? How can prayer be a force in your life?
3. What is the anointing of the Holy Spirit? How do you obtain and keep that anointing?
4. Describe ways in which you can be fervent and persistent in prayer.
5. How have you responded to delays, unanswered prayers and seeming failures of faith in your life?
6. Explain implicit trust and how it relates to mountain-moving faith. Describe a time you experienced this kind of faith.

7. When is it appropriate to exercise commanding faith?
8. Which of Bounds' principles of faith is the most helpful to you? Why?

## READ MORE ABOUT IT

### Biographical

Lyle Wesley Dorsett, *E. M. Bounds: Man of Prayer* (Grand Rapids: Zondervan, 1991)

### Books by E. M. Bounds

*The Complete Works of E. M. Bounds* (Grand Rapids: Baker Book House, 1990)

*Power through Prayer* (Grand Rapids: Baker Book House, 1978)

*Prayer and Praying Men* (Grand Rapids: Baker Book House, 1977)

*Purpose in Prayer* (Chicago: Moody Press, n.d.)

*Winning the Invisible War* (Springdale, Pa.: Whitaker House, 1984)

# 7

# *Andrew Murray*
## (1828–1917)
## *Minister of New Covenant Life*

---

**Faith principle:**

*You can claim your inheritance
promised in the covenant.*

---

Had God not changed Andrew Murray's mind, Murray might have become known as the preacher who tried to stop a revival. He, his father and other ministers of the Dutch Reformed Church had been praying for revival in South Africa for many years, but when it arrived he could not recognize or accept it as being from God. One evening in 1860 Murray was hurriedly summoned by one of his elders to the church where he pastored. The whole congregation had spontaneously begun praying fervently and loudly all at once, totally out of character for a staid, reserved Dutch Reformed church. He tried to exercise his ecclesiastical authority, commanding the congregation, "People, I am your minister sent from God. Silence!" But the people paid no attention to him and kept on praying emotionally and boisterously. Finally out of frustration Murray declared, "God is a God of order, and everything here is confusion," and stalked out of the building.

The prayer meetings continued in spite of Murray's efforts to stifle them. Horrendously, some people even appeared to faint—what today is sometimes called "falling under the power of the Spirit." At a later meeting where he tried to quiet the people, a stranger approached him, advising, "Be careful what you do, for it is the Spirit of God that is at work here. I have just come from America, and this is precisely what I witnessed there."[1] He was referring to the revivals led by Charles Finney and Phoebe Palmer in 1857–1859. This testimony confirmed to Murray the genuineness of the revival. His father, a Dutch Reformed pastor who had prayed for revival for many years, came to visit and assured him, "Andrew, my son, I have longed for such times as these, which the Lord has let you have."[2] From that point on, his way of thinking about the work of the Holy Spirit was transformed, and Andrew supported the revival, which yielded remarkable and lasting results. So the preacher who had tried to resist what he perceived as religious fanaticism became one of those fanatics himself.

## Meet Andrew Murray

Murray would go on to lead other revivals, promote the Holiness movement of the Spirit in South Africa and teach and model a life of faith, respected by people of all theological streams and denominational backgrounds. His teachings and writings have been respected throughout the Christian community for more than a century. His accomplishments demonstrate his life of faith:

- Because of the leadership he displayed and his dynamic, anointed preaching, in the providence of God two years after the revival, at the age of 34, he was elected as moderator of the Dutch Reformed Church of South Africa.

- As a result, he was able to stem the encroaching tide of liberalism and lead his denomination to renewal.

- He authored more than thirty books, many of which continue to be republished and have an enduring impact a century later. Murray's classic books *Absolute Surrender, Abide in Christ* and *With Christ in the School of Prayer* were born out of revivals.

- Due to strain on his vocal chords, he became ill and lost his voice, unable to preach for two years. Yet he experienced miraculous healing and complete restoration of his voice. He then became in his generation one of the primary advocates of divine healing by faith, writing another classic book entitled *Divine Healing*.

Murray's principles of faith echo the teachings of the evangelical leaders we have discussed, as well as adding his own distinctive insights. Let us look at seven faith principles he taught and practiced.

### We Are Partakers of the New Covenant

Andrew Murray's life can be described as a covenant relationship with God. In Murray's spiritual training, the Reformed theology of Dutch and Scottish Calvinism stressed the concept of God's covenant with believers.

Murray expanded upon the traditional idea of Covenant Theology with fresh understanding of the rights and privileges through the New Covenant, which is the last will and testament of Jesus Christ through His death: "Every believer is a child of the New Covenant, and heir to all its promises. The death of the Testator [the person who leaves a will] gives him full right to immediate possession. God longs to bring us into the land of promise; let us not come short through unbelief."[3] For Murray, lack of faith is due to neglect of the covenant. He exhorted, "Believe that every blessing of the covenant of grace is yours; by the death of the Testator you are entitled to it all—and on that faith act, knowing that all is yours."[4] Murray presented four chief covenant principles.

## YOU CAN RECEIVE THE PRIVILEGES OF THE COVENANT

We thus inherit the many provisions of the covenant. Among those covenant blessings through Christ's death, according to Murray, are the following:

Liberty in Christ: "Our New Covenant birthright is to stand in the freedom with which Christ has made us free."[5]

Illumination of the Word of God by the Holy Spirit: "The teaching of God Himself, by the Holy Spirit, to make us understand what He says to us in His Word, is our Covenant right."[6]

The experience of what some call "the baptism of the Spirit" or "the second blessing," a deeper empowering and sanctifying experience. Even though he was not Pentecostal in theology, he liked to call it "the full blessing of Pentecost." Thus, for Murray, "the chief blessing of the covenant is the power of a holy life."[7]

116

*The supernatural life of that covenant through the blood of the cross of Christ:* "Until we learn to form our expectation of a life in the New Covenant, according to the inconceivable worth and power of the blood of God's Son, we never can have even an insight into the entirely supernatural and heavenly life that a child of God may live."[8]

*Physical healing is a divine provision of the atonement as another result of the supernatural covenant life of faith.*[9]

## BUT YOU DO NOT GET ALL YOUR INHERITANCE NOW

While there are some today who teach that the believer can receive his entire inheritance now, Murray explains the difference between the right of inheritance and the possession of that inheritance:

The death of the testator gives the heir immediate right to the inheritance. And yet the heir, if he be a minor, does not enter on the possession. A term of years ends the stage of minority on earth, and he is no longer under guardians. In the spiritual life the state of pupilage ends, not with the expiry of years, but the moment the minor proves his fitness for being made free from the law, by accepting the liberty there is in Christ Jesus.[10]

A believer can, therefore, only inherit what he is mature enough to handle.

## COVENANT FAITH IS BASED ON FELLOWSHIP WITH JESUS, NOT A LEGAL CONTRACT

Some modern teachers of faith have erroneously understood the New Covenant as a legal contract to which God is bound. Murray, however, views the covenant as an intimacy of relationship similar to a marriage covenant or a bond between friends or a parent and child. Murray writes:

> In the face of Jesus, the light which leads to "the full assurance of faith" is always found. To gaze upon His face, to sit still at His feet that the light of His love may shine upon the soul is a sure way of obtaining a strong faith. . . . It is only in living in direct fellowship with Him that our faith can increase and triumph. . . . Those who walk with Him learn from Him to exercise faith.[11]

Our faith is exercised, not in a legal contract, but as a living personal covenant relationship in which God personally speaks His promises to us: "Every exhibition of the power of faith was the fruit of a special revelation from God. . . . Our spiritual power depends on God Himself speaking those promises to us. He speaks to those who walk and live with Him."[12] Murray adds, "Remember that faith is not a logical reasoning which obliges God to act according to His promises. It is, rather, the confident attitude of a child who honors His Father and counts on His love."[13]

Murray emphasizes the importance of intimacy with Christ in prayer and fellowship for strong faith. For Murray, this was especially exemplified and experienced in the Lord's Supper, a time of personal communion with Christ through the New Covenant. His daughter reminisced about those occasions:

> Can one ever forget the times when 500 or 600 communicants would gather around the Lord's Table, and the holy influence of the Lord that permeated the church! Can we forget the holy awe, the deep reverence, the joy and often the rapture written on father's face when "Heaven came down our souls to meet"?
> I remember once that father seemed to have really been taken up to the third heaven and such a deep solemnity

rested on us all before he spoke again with the words, "I live, yet not I, but Christ liveth in me, and that life which I now live in the flesh, I live in *faith*, the faith which is in the Son of God who loved me and gave Himself for me." More especially father emphasized those words "who loved me." Oh the wonder of it that we so little understand! Let us love Him and trust Him more and more!

We left the Table feeling that we had indeed been fed on heavenly manna, and rose with a deeper love and fuller determination to do and dare all for our adorable Lord and Master. We were strengthened and refreshed as with new wine, and in the Thanksgiving Service afterward there was a time of wondrous praise, not from the lips alone, but from the heart.[14]

Partaking of the Lord's Supper today can be a source of strength and faith as we personally experience the love and presence of Christ.

### PUT YOUR FAITH IN THE PROMISER, NOT THE PROMISES

Murray did not put his faith primarily in the promises of God but in God Himself. He exhorts us:

Have faith in God. This faith precedes the faith in the promise of an answer to prayer. The power to believe a promiser depends entirely on faith in the promiser. . . . Faith in the promise is the fruit of faith in the promiser. . . . Let faith focus on God more than on the thing promised, because it is His love, His power, His living presence that will awaken and work the faith. . . . Faith in God fosters faith in the promises.[15]

### *Faith Is Enhanced by the Spirit-Enlivened Word*

Andrew Murray lived constantly in the presence of God. How can we experience that kind of intimacy with God? Murray emphasized the dual role of Scripture and the Holy Spirit for building faith: "As sure as mere knowledge of the Word, by itself, profits but little, so surely faith cannot grow and become strong apart from the Word applied by the Holy Spirit."[16] Our faith is strengthened by repeated meditation upon the Word. But this is not the role of Scripture only: "The personal application of the general promises of the Word to our specific needs is given to us by the leading of the Holy Spirit. . . . The quickening of the Word by the Spirit comes only from within, not from without."[17] He encourages us, "Let the Word create around you, create within you a holy atmosphere, a holy, heavenly light, in which your soul will be refreshed and strengthened for the work of daily life."[18] Murray lived in that "holy atmosphere," being caught up in the presence of God, and so can you through the Spirit and the Word of God.

### Exercise the Faith That Takes

Andrew Murray's life shows us that he practiced a faith that has both a passive and an active side. He devotes one whole devotional book, *Waiting on God*, to understanding the importance of being still and listening quietly for the voice of God. Yet he also writes of "the faith that takes."[19] His study of the Greek New Testament revealed that the word for "receive" by faith means an active taking hold of, not a passive acceptance. So Murray explained that once we know the will of the Lord from the Word of God and the leading of the Holy Spirit, we can take hold of the promises of God by faith and stand confidently on those promises. Elijah had to pray seven times, even though he was certain rain would come—taking hold of the promises of God by faith may involve continued, persevering prayer.[20]

## Faith Plants Seeds of Praise and Confession

Similar to the positive confession teaching of Charles
Spurgeon, Phoebe Palmer and Hannah Whitall Smith,
Murray exhorts, "Praise the Lord without waiting to feel
better, or to have more faith. Praise Him, and say with
David, 'O Lord, I cried unto Thee and Thou hast healed
me' (Ps. 30:2)."[21] He counsels us not to waste time be-
moaning our unbelief but rather to put our eyes on Jesus,
confessing unbelief and doing away with it once and for
all. He advises us not to spend time brooding over our
problems but rather to speak by faith and confess the
Scriptures. Murray encourages us to exercise our faith
as a "seed-word." In other words, exercising the measure
of faith we have through words of positive confession
of the Word of God and thanksgiving, no matter how
small it may seem, will germinate and produce fruit.
He emphasizes our role in activating the will of God:
"God has made the execution of His will dependent on
the will of man. His promises will be fulfilled as much
as our faith allows."[22]

This may appear similar to some modern faith teaching that warns against ever making a negative confession. However, for classic faith teachers like Murray,
a negative confession may be a positive thing when it
causes the believer to deal with reality. Contrary to some
modern teaching, according to Murray, part of proper
confession is admitting to the Lord your unbelief; then
asking the Lord to give you faith. Murray recommends
to others the confession he made:

> Lord, I am still aware of the unbelief which is in me. I
> find it difficult to believe that I am assured of my heal-
> ing just because I possess Him who works it in me. And,
> nevertheless, I want to conquer the unbelief. You, Lord,
> will give me the victory. I *desire* to believe, I *will* believe,

and by Your grace, I *can* believe. Yes, Lord, I believe, for You help me with my unbelief.[23]

## You Can Exercise Spiritual Authority and Power

As a young pastor in the wilderness of South Africa, Andrew Murray made it a habit to visit his parishioners. On one occasion he was riding on horseback to visit a family in the bush. He stopped to give his horse a rest and dismounted. Soon the horse picked up the scent of wild dogs and bolted in fear, leaving Andrew behind. The wild dogs approached Andrew, snarling, but there was nowhere he could go. He believed God had called him on this mission and prayed that He would protect him. With faith and boldness, he walked through the midst of the pack of dogs. They continued to growl threateningly and bite at him but did not touch him.[24]

On another occasion several years later, when Murray was preaching boldly about the use and abuse of alcohol and the need for temperance, he was threatened. Yet he continued to take a stand fearlessly, claiming by faith the protection of the Lord. One day someone carried through the threats and tried to torch his house. But the curtains did not catch fire, and the house was protected from harm.

Where did Murray acquire such faith and boldness? Just a few years earlier, as a seminary student in Holland, he made a trip to Germany and became acquainted with Johann Blumhardt, the Lutheran Pietist pastor who had become renowned for his pioneering work in spiritual warfare, casting out demons and ministry of healing. Murray became convinced that the power of God is operative today and can be obtained through prayer and faith. Decades later he quoted J. Hudson Taylor's statement about Christians being a supernatural people born again by a supernatural birth, kept by a supernatural power, sustained on supernatural food, taught by a supernatural Teacher from a supernatural Book. Murray believed that the signs of Mark 16 are applicable to all times and all the spiritual graces are promised to us today.

Similar to Spurgeon and Bounds, Andrew Murray speaks of Christ Himself as "a living force . . . animating and enlightening us and filling our lives," flowing out of our communion with Christ.[25] Murray likewise combines the forces of prayer and faith, comparing them to the mighty torrent of water released from a dam: "Real faith can never be disappointed. It knows how to exercise its power, it must be gathered up, just like water, until the stream can come down in full force. Prayer must often be 'heaped up' until God sees that its measure is full. Then the answer comes."[26]

Murray also believed in and exercised the right of the believer to exercise power of attorney in the name of Jesus. He advocates the authority of the believer in this prayer: "Grant especially, blessed Lord, that your Church might believe that it is by the power of united prayer that she can bind and loose in heaven, cast out Satan, save souls, remove mountains, and hasten the coming of the kingdom."[27]

## Healing Is a Provision of Covenant Faith

At the height of his career Andrew Murray's faith in the supernatural power of God was tested to its greatest limit. He had been preaching and conducting evangelistic and missions tours in many locations, speaking several times a day. His voice was becoming strained, so he went to see a doctor. The doctor commanded him sternly to cease preaching immediately or he would lose his voice. Murray felt constrained to honor his preaching commitments, and as a result he lost his voice for almost two years. How difficult it was for a dynamic, successful preacher who loved to teach the Word of God to be silenced.

During this time, though he could not speak, Murray read and wrote extensively, producing new materials. He would write his address to a conference and someone else would deliver it. Though he was not aware of sin in his life, for Murray it was a time of spiritual soul-searching. Emerging from this time of reflection Murray laid down this principle: "The more we give ourselves to experience personally sanctification by faith, the more we shall also experience healing by faith."[28]

Eventually Murray visited the Bethshan Healing Home in London, staying there for three weeks, seeking God and meditating upon the Word of God in an atmosphere of faith and peace. He received counsel and prayer from Pastor Otto Stockmayer, the Swiss pastor who began a ministry of healing homes for the purpose of providing a spiritually therapeutic atmosphere. He was gradually but miraculously healed, never to have serious trouble with his voice again. Rather, in his later years, even when his body was frail and weak, his voice boomed out strongly. Soon after his healing he wrote his book *Divine Healing*, as well as other writings on healing. His principles issue both out of his experience and sound theological reflection.

### IT IS GOD'S WILL TO HEAL

Murray struggled for some time over whether he should even pray for healing, wondering if the infirmity was more of a blessing than health was. Eventually, though, Murray became convinced that it is God's will to heal. That is a vital key, Murray realized, to appropriating healing. Later, after his healing, he wrote in reference to his former belief:

It is a prevalent idea that piety is easier in sickness than in health, and that silent suffering inclines the soul to seek the Lord more than the distractions of life. For these reasons, sick people hesitate to ask for healing from the Lord. They believe that sickness may be more of a blessing to them than health. To think thus is to ignore that healing and its fruits are divine. . . . Although many sick people may have glorified God by their patience in suffering, He can be still more glorified by a health which He has sanctified.[29]

He found from his own experience that passively praying "if it be God's will" can sometimes hinder God's will from being done.[30]

Murray thus concluded that healing is a provision of the blood atonement of Christ through the covenant: "The body also shares in the redemption effected by Christ."[31] Therefore, we have a covenant right to healing, according to James 5, because "healing and health form part of Christ's salvation."[32] This does not mean that we can claim perfect health in this life but that we can receive a foretaste of heaven even in our mortal bodies.

### DISCERN THE ROOT REASONS FOR THE ILLNESS

Before a person can be healed, Murray counsels from his own experience, he must discern the root causes of the illness and God's reason for allowing the illness: "If one is sick and desires healing, it is of prime importance that the true cause of the sickness be discovered. This is always the first step toward recovery. If the particular cause is not recognized, and attention is directed toward subordinate causes, or to supposed but not real causes, healing is out of the question."[33]

Once we know the spiritual roots of sickness, Murray counsels, "One of the chief benefits, then, of divine healing is to teach us that our body ought to be set free from the yoke of our own will to become the Lord's property."[34] He explains:

> This life of attention and action, of renouncement and of crucifixion, constitutes a holy life. The Lord first brings it to us in the form of sickness, making us understand what we are lacking. He then shows us by our healing [*sic*], which calls the soul to a life of continual attention to the voice of God. Most Christians see nothing more in divine healing than a temporal blessing for the body, while in the promise of our holy God, its end is to make us holy.[35]

Murray thus believed there is a close link between our holiness and receiving healing.

### DISCERN GOD'S WILL IN DELAY OR LACK OF HEALING

From his own experience Murray recognized that God may have a purpose in delaying healing: "God does not grant healing to our prayers until He has attained the end for which He had permitted the sickness. He wills that this discipline bring us into a more intimate communion with Him. . . . God's timing is perfect. He can delay anything as He sees necessary, and then more speedily bring the answer at just the right moment."[36]

On the other hand, we may need to persevere in faith, because delays in answers to prayer are intended to prove and strengthen our faith. Sometimes it is due to the opposition of Satan, who attempts to hinder answers to prayer, as in Daniel 10:12–13. In such cases, Murray counsels, "The only means by which this unseen enemy can be conquered is faith. Standing firmly on the promises of God, faith refuses to yield, continuing to pray and wait for the answer, even when it is delayed, knowing that the victory is sure (Ephesians 6:12–13)."[37] Contrary to some who claim a person should pray just once, in these situations Murray encourages repeated and continual prayer.[38]

While Murray believed that God's general will is healing, he also understood that God may reveal upon occasion that in His sovereignty He has other plans:

> If the Lord had some other arrangement in mind for His children whom He was about to call home to Him, He would make His will known to them. By His Holy Spirit, He would give them a desire to depart. In other special cases, He would awaken some special conviction. As a general rule, however, the Word of God promises us healing in answer to the prayer of faith.[39]

Murray further explains, "The man of faith places himself under the direction of the Spirit, which will enable him to discern the will of God regarding him, if something should prevent his attaining the age of seventy. Just as it is on earth, every rule in heaven has its exceptions."[40] In other words, a believer should pray for and expect healing unless God shows otherwise.

### GOD USES DOCTORS AND MEDICINE, AS WELL AS DIVINE HEALING

Andrew Murray was not opposed to doctors and medicine, but he believed that Jesus Himself is the first, best and greatest Physician.[41] Murray himself throughout his life sometimes relied solely on God for healing, and at other times made use of doctors and medicine. One time, during one of his evangelistic tours, Murray was thrown from a cart and broke his arm. He prayed for God's healing, bandaged his arm and applied cold compresses; then he preached that evening! Sometime later he showed the arm to a doctor friend, who was amazed and commented that it was "most remarkably and perfectly set and healed."[42] Yet on other occasions of illness or accident he received medical treatment from doctors. Regarding the use of medicine Murray advises, "Does the use of remedies [medicine] exclude the prayer of faith? To this we believe the reply should be no, for the experience of a large number of believers testifies that, in answer to their prayer, God has often blessed the use of remedies, and made them a means of healing."[43] Still, Murray considered the prayer of faith without medicine is the best way to obtain the grace of God. His counsel is as timely today as it was more than a century ago: "Let the Word of God be your guide in this matter. . . . Seek to know what God Himself speaks to you in His Word."[44]

### GET YOUR ATTENTION OFF YOURSELF

Murray's concern was to trust God first and get attention off self: "When we use earthly remedies for healing, all the attention of the sick one is on the body. Divine healing, however, calls us to turn our attention away from the body, abandoning ourselves—soul and body—to the Lord's care, occupying ourselves with Him alone."[45] Murray understood that any preoccupation with one's illness, including preoccupation with doctors and medicine, can be a stumbling block to healing: "Then the first thing to learn is to cease to be anxious about the state of your body. You have trusted it to the Lord, and He has taken responsibility." When we learn to trust the Lord, "we learn to relinquish the care of our health entirely to Him. The smallest indication of the return of the sickness is regarded as a warning not to consider our body, but to be occupied with the Lord only."[46] Allowing our minds to dwell on our pains can hinder the healing process.

## STRENGTHEN YOUR FAITH THROUGH A POINT OF CONTACT

You might be surprised to know that the concept of using a "point of contact" to express or release one's faith does not originate with Oral Roberts but is at least as old as Andrew Murray. In 1884 Murray wrote in his book *Divine Healing* that the laying on of hands and anointing with oil should be regarded "not as a remedy, but as a pledge of the mighty virtue of the Holy Spirit, as a means of strengthening faith, a *point of contact* and of communion between the sick one and members of the Church who are called to anoint him with oil."[47] A point of contact is not magical or occultic. Murray explains that we must personally come in contact with the healing touch of Christ: "Let each contact with the blood be contact with the Lamb, more particularly with His gentleness and meekness. Let your faith touch just the hem of His garment and power will go out from Him."[48]

### *The Greatest Faith Is Exercised through Self-Denial*

Just as for healing, we must take attention off ourselves, so Murray also asserts that if we do not practice self-denial and let go of the world, we cannot exercise faith.[49] Moreover, Murray taught that self-denial goes to the "very deepest roots of the life of faith. The deeper we are willing to enter into the death of self, the more shall we know of the mighty power of God, and the perfect blessedness of a perfect trust."[50] Like Müller, he understood that "difficulties are the proving ground of faith; they give it nourishment and strength."[51] Although it is ultimately Christ's work to increase faith, Andrew Murray gives this qualification: "Let there only be an undivided surrender to the Lord Jesus, the sacrifice of the 'self' life—'I'—in order to walk with Him; in that walk unbelief will wither."[52]

## You, Too, Can Enter Your Promised Land!

Andrew Murray shows us that a person can be led of God to bring revival and renewal to a whole denomination. His life of faith was respected by people of other denominations and theological viewpoints as well—Presbyterians and Anglicans, as well as Baptists like Charles Spurgeon and F. B. Meyer. You can pray this prayer of faith and consecration by Andrew Murray and enter into the Promised Land of your covenant inheritance:

> Father, show me the way to that promised land where You bring Your people to have them wholly for Yourself. I will abandon everything to follow You, to hold converse with You alone, in order that You may fill me with Your blessing. Lord, let Your word, "I will bless thee," live in my heart as a Word of God. Then I will give myself wholly to live for others and to be a blessing. Amen.[53]

### THINK AND DISCUSS

1. Describe God's covenant with believers. Explain your rights, privileges and responsibilities in covenant with God.
2. How does Scripture strengthen your faith?
3. Explain Murray's phrase "faith takes." In what ways can you "take" by faith?
4. How does "seed faith" or "sowing and reaping" work? What seeds of faith can you plant?

5. How can you exercise spiritual authority and power?
6. Discuss Murray's principles of healing. Do you agree or disagree with them? Why?
7. Which healing principles are the most meaningful to you?
8. How can self-denial be an expression of great faith?
9. Which of Murray's principles of faith is most helpful to you? Why?

## READ MORE ABOUT IT

### Biographical

Leona Choy, *Andrew and Emma Murray: An Intimate Portrait of Their Marriage and Ministry* (Winchester, Va.: Golden Morning Publishing, 2000)

William M. Douglas, *Andrew Murray and His Message* (Grand Rapids: Baker Book House, 1981)

### Books by Andrew Murray

*The Blood of the Cross* (Springdale, Pa.: Whitaker House, 1981)

*Divine Healing* (Springdale, Pa.: Whitaker House, 1982)

*With Christ in the School of Prayer* (Springdale, Pa.: Whitaker House, 1982)

*The Inner Life* (Springdale, Pa.: Whitaker House, 1984)

*The Prayer Life* (Basingstoke, UK: Marshall, Morgan & Scott, 1968)

*The Two Covenants* (Ft. Washington, Pa.: Christian Literature Crusade, 1974)

## Devotional Books by Andrew Murray

M. J. Shepperson, compiler, *Day by Day with Andrew Murray* (Minneapolis: Bethany Fellowship, 1961)
*God's Best Secrets* (Grand Rapids: Zondervan, 1971)

# 8

## A. B. Simpson
### (1843–1919)

## Leader of Visionary Faith

---

**Faith principle:**

*Holy Christ-centered faith
leads to wholeness of life.*

---

Young Presbyterian minister Albert Benjamin Simpson possessed an evangelistic fervor and a growing interest in missions. One night while sleeping he experienced a dramatic and haunting dream that would drive his life and ministry from that point on. Simpson recalled vividly:

> I was awakened one night from sleep, trembling with a strange and solemn sense of God's overshadowing power, and on my soul was burning the remembrance of a strange dream through which I had at that moment come. It seemed to me that I was sitting in a vast auditorium and millions of people were sitting there

around me. All the Christians in the world seemed to be there, and on the platform was a great multitude of faces and forms. They seemed to be mostly Chinese. They were not speaking, but in mute anguish were wringing their hands, and their faces wore an expression I can never forget. As I woke with that vision on my mind, I trembled with the Holy Spirit, and I threw myself on my knees, and every fibre in my being answered, "Yes, Lord, I will go."[1]

Although Simpson himself never actually served on a mission field, this dream launched within him a grand missionary vision. That dream expanded into a worldwide ministry, both for himself and the missionary organization he founded—The Christian and Missionary Alliance (C&MA). The C&MA has grown to four million adherents worldwide in more than fifty countries and become a missions-oriented denomination.

## Meet A. B. Simpson

For more than forty years Simpson's visionary faith carried him on eagle's wings with incredible creative energy and anointing through the Holy Spirit. A popular speaker and prolific writer, he published more than a hundred books. Among the ministries he initiated included the following:

- street preaching
- ministry to prostitutes
- ministry to ethnic groups
- Sunday evening evangelistic services (forerunner of the 1990s Saturday night seeker services)
- weekly healing services and a healing home

- Christian restaurant ministry (forerunner of the 1960s coffeehouse ministry)
- dozens of new songs

This is not to say that all of Simpson's innovations were successful or accepted. Due to his flair for the dramatic and emotional he was sarcastically called an "enthusiast." Because of his belief in divine healing he was considered by some as a radical faith healer and ridiculed as a quack miracle worker. Nevertheless, as he grew in faith and overcame the obstacles, he became one of the most renowned preachers and greatest advocates of his day of a supernatural walk of faith and holiness. Evangelist Dwight L. Moody held Simpson in high esteem, remarking, "No one gets to my heart like that man."

Simpson emphasized what he called "the full gospel," a fourfold gospel of presenting Jesus Christ as "Savior, Sanctifier, Healer and Coming King." He was driven by a desire for the higher Christian life of faith, holiness, wholeness and anticipation of preparing for the second coming of Christ. His mission statement reflected his vision of worldwide evangelization:

- To hold up Jesus in His fullness, "the same yesterday, and today, and forever!"
- To lead God's hungry children to know their full inheritance of privilege and blessing for spirit, soul and body.
- To encourage and incite the people of God to do the neglected work of our age and time among the unchurched classes at home and the perishing heathen abroad.[2]

To accomplish his vision, unlike Andrew Murray, Simpson was not able to remain within his denominational structure but found he needed to launch a new interdenominational parachurch organization. He felt a burden to reach out to those who "felt themselves alienated from the formal church, but not from the Lord."[3] Through his evangelistic efforts in New York City, he converted a hundred Italian immigrants, but his high-society church would not accept them into membership. As a result, he related, "I left my church to form a church for the people of all classes based on absolute freedom."[4] He stepped out in faith without a denomination or funds to support him. In fact, in his integrity, he refused to allow people to split from his former church in order to join him. Instead, he started a work from scratch on the streets of New York. Rather than trying to bring people to church, Simpson sought ways to bring the church to the people. He was on the forefront of what today would be similar to the "seeker-friendly" methodology of evangelism.

Probably more than any other classic evangelical leader, Simpson addressed the questions and issues of a sound and strong faith. He built upon and expanded the teachings and practices of earlier leaders of faith such as Müller, Spurgeon, Hudson Taylor and Phoebe Palmer. As a contemporary of Andrew Murray, though continents apart, Simpson's life and teachings parallel remarkably those of Murray.[5] What made Simpson such a man of visionary faith? Let us look at six of his principles of holy Christ-centered faith.

### Claim Your Inheritance for the Whole Person— Spirit, Soul and Body

Like Murray, Simpson believed that we have an inheritance as believers. He pictured the Church as spiritual Israel, today destined to enter a spiritual Promised Land. Further, Simpson taught that our inheritance is primarily spiritual but includes material blessings as well:

> So our inheritance is all the fullness of God's exceedingly great and precious promises: all the unclaimed wealth of these forty thousand checks in the Bank Book of the Bible—promises for the soul, promises for the body, promises for ourselves, promises for others, promises for our work, promises for our trials, promises for time, and promises for eternity.[6]

Like Murray, Simpson recognized that we receive only a "*sample* of the inheritance of glory which Christ has purchased for us."[7] He also explained that God sovereignly puts limits on His blessings for His purposes and our good: "He exercises a loving oversight in His blessings; and while He freely gives to all who ask and trust Him . . . yet even when He gives most largely it is in the line which His wisdom and love see most consistent with our highest good and His supreme glory."[8]

### YOU ARE NEVER UNPROSPEROUS

Although these promises include physical and material blessings, Simpson's emphasis, unlike some prosperity promoters today, was centered upon prosperity for fulfilling God's work, not for self:

> There is no Christian who cannot claim and exercise the very power of God . . . for everything connected with His cause, and our ministry shall touch every part of His work. . . . The removing of obstacles, the influencing of human hearts and minds, the bringing together of workers, the obtaining of helpers, the supply of financial needs; all these are proper subjects for believing prayer

137

and proper lines for demonstrating the all-sufficiency of God.[9]

Similar to many in the prosperity movement today, Simpson cited 3 John 2 as God's desire for the Church: "I pray that in all respects you may prosper and be in good health, just as your soul prospers" (NASB). However, unlike some today, he maintained that health and prosperity are a part of *holy* wholeness, related to the spiritual and emotional state of the soul. For Simpson, while prosperity can include material blessings, that is not the chief emphasis: "There is no harm whatever in having money, houses, lands, friends and children *if* you do not value these things or ones for themselves."[10]

Rather than striving for prosperity, Simpson stressed contentment. He declared that he was *never* "unprosperous," even in times when he appeared to lack. For Simpson, the key to receiving blessing from God is attitude: "When you become satisfied with God . . . everything else so loses its charm that He can give it to you without harm. Then you can take just as much as you choose and use it for His glory. . . . Then every bank, stock, and investment will be but a channel through which you can pour out His benevolence and extend His grace."[11]

## MAINTAIN HOLY INDIFFERENCE FOR THE EARTHLY

Simpson stressed the "discipline of prosperity," that working of God in our hearts to maintain a godly attitude when we do prosper:

How few Christians really know how to abound. How frequently prosperity changes their temper and the habits and fruits of their lives! To receive God's blessing in temporal things, to have wealth suddenly thrust upon us, to be surrounded with the congenial friends, to be enriched with all the happiness that love, home, the

world's applause and unbounded prosperity can give,
and yet to keep a humble heart, to be separated from
the world in its spirit and in its pleasures, to keep our
hearts in holy indifference from the love and need of
earthly things . . . and to use our prosperity and wealth
as a sacred trust for Him, counting nothing our own,
and still depending upon Him as simply as in the days
of penury—this, indeed, is an experience rarely found,
and only possible through the infinite grace of God.[12]

This counsel provides the balance and maturity needed
to address the "Health and Wealth Gospel" of today.
People of truly great faith will have a "holy indifference"
toward material prosperity.

### Accentuate the Positive, and Avoid the Negative

Taking his cue from other classic evangelical leaders like Charles Spurgeon, Hannah Whitall Smith and
Phoebe Palmer, Simpson expanded upon the idea that
confession of our faith and the Word of God is vital. In
fact, he insisted, "Faith will die without confession."[13]
Like Palmer, Simpson believed that faith confesses the
blessing, but it does not mean that you can possess anything you confess. Contrary to some modern positive
confession teachers, for Simpson, confessing one's faith
is not merely repeating a Scripture or formula. Rather,
it is unfailingly bearing witness of Christ and confessing
not riches and possessions but rather God's faithfulness,
the promises of God, healing and especially the Word of
God. There is great power in confessing the blessings of
God when our motives and heart are pure.

For Simpson, just as a positive godly confession
can work mightily to strengthen faith and accomplish
God's purposes, so also negative attitudes, words and
thoughts can hinder the exercise of faith and the recep-

tion of blessing and healing. These may be manifested through wrong thoughts, unbelief, fear, discouragement or complaining.

Such thoughts not only affect us spiritually but infect the whole personality—mind, emotions and body:

> If you want to keep the health of Christ, keep from all spiritual sores, from all heart-wounds and irritations. One hour of fretting will wear out more vitality than a week of work, and one minute of malignity, or wrangling jealousy or envy will hurt more than a drink of poison. Sweetness of spirit and joyousness of heart are essential to full health. . . . We do not wonder that some people have poor health when we hear them talk for half an hour. They have enough dislikes, prejudices, doubts and fears to exhaust the strongest constitution. Beloved, if you would keep God's life and strength, keep out of the things that kill it.[14]

From such negative thoughts, unbelief, fear, discouragement and depression can set in to paralyze faith. In contrast, one of Simpson's most devoted rescue mission workers, Sophie Lichtenfels, worked as a common scrubwoman. Nonetheless, in spite of her lowly position, she recognized her high position in Christ and heartily practiced Simpson's principles of making positive confessions and avoiding negative attitudes. She became well known for her joyful encouragement of everyone around her.[15]

### Faith Is Activated by Connecting with God

Simpson declared that God works in cooperation with man's faith:

> We must trust as if all depended upon God and we must work as if all depended on us. . . . The blessings which

God has to impart to us through the Lord Jesus Christ do not wait upon some sovereign act of His will, but are already granted, completed and prepared and simply awaiting the contact of a believing hand to open all the channels of communication.[16]

He compared it to activating the electric current to a light bulb by turning on the switch.

Contrary to some teaching that encourages people to step out in faith unconditionally, Simpson cautions to wait and be sure before acting in faith. He encourages believers not to feel guilty for waiting for the sure word:

> God is not displeased with us for waiting until He gives us ample assurance of His will, so that when we step out it may be irrevocable. . . . The one thing in which Gideon's act is unmistakably clear as a pattern for us is in the fact of his becoming certain before stepping forward. The secret of faith and victory is to be sure of our way and then go forward unfalteringly.[17]

It was Simpson's practice to get quiet and separate himself from the distracting influences in order to hear God's voice. He did not just step out on faith indiscriminately, but only when God gave clear indication:

> Whenever faith can clearly know that He has spoken, all it has to do is to lay the whole responsibility on Him and go forward. . . . To all who wait upon His will the Master gives some word of faith for the future. . . . It is most essential in our conflicts of faith that we have a sure word of prophecy on which to rest, otherwise our struggle will be a very perplexing one.[18]

To those with an illness or injury, Simpson counseled, "Do not rise from your bed or walk on your lame foot because somebody tells you to do so. That is not faith, but impression."[19] Once we do receive a clear word from God, we can go forward in faith without doubting.

## Faith Exercises Discernment

On matters of faith, healing and supernatural manifestations, Simpson has become known as an "apostle of balance." He believed in and encouraged the supernatural power of God decades before the Pentecostal movement, but when the movement arose in 1906 he also exhorted believers to exercise discernment. He neither accepted unconditionally all of the tenets and practices of the Pentecostal movement, nor did he condemn the movement altogether. Simpson believed in the supernatural gifts of the Spirit like tongues, prophecy and healing. Yet he also perceived from the Spirit and experience that such manifestations can be from God, from Satan, from the flesh or from an imperfect mixture of flesh and Spirit.

While Simpson affirmed that we can receive genuine divine impulses, he also gave caution not to accept all such urges as the voice of God:

> God does give us impressions but not with the intent that we should act on them as impressions. If the impression comes from God, He will Himself give sufficient evidence to establish it beyond the possibility of a doubt. . . . We are not to ignore the Shepherd's personal voice, but like Paul and his companions at Troas we are to listen to all the voices that speak and gather from all the circumstances, as they did, the full mind of the Lord.[20]

Too often, Simpson observed, a person thinks he is receiving a revelation from the Lord when it is really an impression from the fleshly nature.[21] Simpson counseled discernment through experience and maturity. According to him, prophecy can also be counterfeited and needs to be tested. He warned that seeking after prophetic words can become a distorted form of Christian fortune-telling.

## Holy Faith Leads to Wholeness

Less than a year apart, both Simpson and Murray experienced the healing power of God. In 1881 Simpson visited a summer camp resort in Old Orchard, Maine, where Dr. Charles Cullis, a physician with a divine healing ministry, was speaking. Simpson's heart and nerves were failing, and he walked with weakness and pain. His doctor did not think he had much time to live. Simpson was cautious and unsure about this "faith healing" teaching and did not respond to an invitation to receive prayer for healing. Rather, he spent time seeking God and His Word to find out for himself on the Friday afternoon of the conference. He recalled, "It drove me to my Bible. . . . I am so glad I did not go to man. At His feet alone, with my Bible open, and with no one to help or guide me, I became convinced that this was part of Christ's glorious Gospel for a sinful and suffering world, for all who would believe and receive His word. That was enough."[22] A. W. Tozer vividly describes how Simpson came to experience divine healing:

> He walked out under the open sky, painfully, slowly, for he was always weak and out of breath in those days. A path into a pine wood invited him like an open door into a cathedral. There on a carpet of soft pine needles, with a fallen log for an altar, while the wind through the trees played an organ voluntary, he knelt and sought the face of his God.

Suddenly the power of God came upon him. It seemed as if God Himself was beside him, around him, filling all the fragrant sanctuary with the glory of His presence.[23]

There beneath the "green vaulted ceiling," he raised his hand toward heaven and made his pledge to God to take Christ as his healer.[24] He remarked of the moment, "Every fibre in my soul was tingling with the sense of God's presence."[25] Within days he climbed a 3,000-foot mountain, enabled by the energizing of the Lord.

As a result of Simpson's miraculous healing, he wrote and preached extensively on faith and healing. Consequently, he became one of the leading teachers on what could be considered the "classic faith movement" of the late nineteenth and early twentieth centuries. He walked in divine healing and health for nearly forty years. Simpson's principles of healing parallel and supplement those of Murray, providing sound practical counsel for health and healing today.

### HEALING FAITH COMES FROM HOLY ABIDING WITH CHRIST

Key to Simpson's healing and his transformed vigor was his close walk with God and seeking Him wholly. He wrote from his own experience, "It is from close and trustful confidence alone that we can claim His healing. . . . We must get under His very wings and in the bosom of His love before faith can claim its highest victories in our inmost being. . . . This is the secret of divine healing. It is union with the One who is our physical Head as well as the source of our spiritual life."[26]

In times of illness Simpson advised, like Murray, to get the focus off our self and striving to be healed. He cautioned that we should not focus on trying to be healed: "Some suffering Christians have been so anxious to get well and have spent so much time in trying to claim healing, that they have lost their spiritual blessing. God sometimes has to teach such persons that there must be a willingness to be sick before they are yielded enough to receive His fullest blessing."[27]

### RECOGNIZE GOD'S HOLY PURPOSES IN ALLOWING SICKNESS

Simpson did not accept the old medieval belief that God makes people sick to make them holy; however, contrary to some modern teaching, Simpson did assert, "God uses sickness. God uses trial. He lets the devil have a part in it, but it is by God's permission that all this has come."[28] Simpson observed from years of healing services as well as his own experience, "We shall often find that God is dealing with men and women through their very sickness and we want to be careful first to get them into harmony with His will and spiritually prepared for the blessing of healing."[29] Simpson described how some believers receive healing in their earlier Christian experiences:

> . . . but when we meet them a little later in their life, we often find them struggling with sickness, unhealed and unable to understand the reason of their failure. It is because God is leading them into a deeper spiritual experience. He is teaching them to understand His guidance, and some people cannot be guided any other way than by a touch of pain. . . . God is teaching them His finer touches.[30]

In these situations God wants to effect a "deeper healing." One of those "finer touches" for Simpson occurred in 1911. While visiting Central America, he contracted a tropical fever, from which he recovered after a time. He believed God was teaching him through this experience to identify with the sufferings of missionaries.

Like many other classic evangelical leaders such as A. J. Gordon, Andrew Murray, R. A. Torrey and Oswald Chambers, Simpson taught that healing is a provision for all believers through the atonement, yet God in His mysterious divine purposes may not heal all. Although, like Murray, Simpson believed it is generally God's will for a believer to live for seventy to eighty years, he also acknowledged that in God's sovereign will a person may die young:

> Sometimes the Master is taking home His child and will He not, in such cases, lift the veil and show the trusting heart that its service is done? How often He does! A dear young girl in Michigan who for some time claimed healing, awoke one day from sleep, her face covered with the reflection of heaven, and told her loved ones that the Master had led her to trust for life thus far, but now was taking her to Himself. It is well, and let no one dare to reproach such a heart with unfaithfulness.[31]

Unlike some who would scold the child or parents for unbelief, Simpson recognized that her death at a young age was the sovereign will of God. Simpson, along with many other evangelical leaders, believed that it was generally God's will to heal, unless God revealed otherwise.

### MAINTAIN A JOYFUL SPIRIT

Simpson's principles of avoiding a negative attitude and maintaining a positive confession of faith are especially vital for healing:

> A flash of ill temper, a cloud of despondency, an impure thought or desire can poison your blood, inflame your tissues, disturb your nerves and interrupt the whole process of God's life in your body! On the other hand, the spirit of joy, freedom from anxious care and worry, a generous and loving heart, the sedative of peace, the uplifting influence of hope and confidence—these are

better than pills, stimulants and sedatives . . . making it true in a literal as well as a spiritual sense, that "the joy of the Lord is your strength."[32]

In his pamphlet *How to Receive Divine Healing* Simpson advised, "Don't expect to have a spell of weariness and reaction," but rather "just go calmly forward . . . expecting Him to give you the necessary strength to carry you through."[33]

### Abandon Medical Treatment Only If God Has Given Special Faith

One of the most controversial practices concerning divine healing is expressing faith through the abandoning of medicine and doctors. For more than thirty years Simpson himself personally never took medicine nor received treatment from a doctor, except for cough drops for his throat, and eyeglasses. On one occasion, while he was preaching in Pittsburgh at Carnegie Hall, he pulled out his handkerchief and several cough drops fell out of his pocket, rattling "like marbles all over the platform!"[34]

Although Simpson never had medical treatment, he did not disparage those who did. On the contrary, he counseled people to use medical means unless God had clearly given them special faith to do otherwise: "If you have any question about your faith for this, make it a special matter of preparation and prayer. Ask God to give you special faith for this act. . . . Act your faith . . . not to show your faith, or display your courage, but *because* of your faith, begin to act as one that is healed. . . . But it is most important that you should be careful that you *do not do this on any other human faith or word.*"[35]

Faith healer John Alexander Dowie wanted Simpson to team up with him to promote divine healing, but Simpson did not share his theology or emphasis on healing, especially Dowie's condemnation of using doctors and medicine. As a result, Dowie opposed Simpson's ministry and traveled to Pittsburgh to conduct a series of meetings for the express purpose of condemning Simpson. While eating dinner before the opening lecture Dowie choked on a fish bone and was unable to carry on the meetings. When Simpson was told about the incident, he commented, "Oh, Dowie. Yes, I committed that man to God long ago."[36]

### GOD MAY GRANT STRENGTH RATHER THAN TOTAL HEALING

Contrary to some modern teaching that a person need never be sick, Simpson taught, "God never promised there will be no disease, but if disease comes it will be overcome." "Overcoming" to Simpson meant that God provides the power to gain victory even when healing does not come. There were times when Simpson became ill and did not receive instantaneous healing, yet God enabled him to carry on. He found daily strength through abiding in Christ in order to complete his daily tasks, even when humanly he was weak, especially in the last years of his life.

Simpson did not berate a person for deficiency of faith if no healing occurred. Rather, he encouraged people to plant and cultivate even the smallest seed of faith: "The smallest grain of faith is a deathless and incorruptible germ that will yet plant the heavens and cover the heavens with harvest of imperishable glory."[37]

### ACCEPT WITH DIGNITY THE TIME TO DIE

Like Spurgeon, Simpson declared that a man is immortal until his work is done. Health until death like a ripe apple falling off a tree is an ideal, though not a promise of God. Simpson acknowledged what some contemporary faith teaching fails to understand: that a person can die of a sickness with dignity:

> It is a beautiful picture of faith that even infirmity and approaching dissolution cannot subdue or even cloud, reminding us that the Christian's last hours may be his brightest and that the sublimest triumphs of his life should be in the face even of his foes. Have we not all seen such victories, in which the withering frame and worn out forces of nature and the very frailty of the outward temple made it more transparent to the glory that was shining out from within.[38]

To Simpson, then, death from a sickness may not be unbelief or poverty of faith but may actually involve operation of a mighty faith. That is a classic faith theology of death. Death, even from illness, can be for the Christian a triumph. Simpson's own health fell short of his ideal, but he maintained a life of victory even in sickness and death. He remained quite healthy into his seventies, but in the last two or three years of his life he suffered a stroke accompanied by periods of weakness, melancholy and loss of memory. Just days before his death, missionary statesman Robert Jaffray and other leaders assembled around him to claim healing. The aged sage remarked to them, "Boys, I can't go that far with you this time."[39] He knew his time was drawing to an end and that God had not given him faith to claim healing. Still, he testified, "Jesus is so real." He knew that he, like the apostle Paul, had completed his course and his task was finished.

### The Greatest Faith Is Christ-Centered

Simpson's ultimate message stressed that faith, whether for healing or financial needs or blessings, is Christ-centered—what he called "the Christ life." For

Simpson, Jesus working in us maintains "the highest Christian life." Faith seeks to glorify Jesus, not self. Faith seeks more of God, not more blessings.

For Simpson, faith and holiness work together. The life of faith ultimately is demonstrated in victory over sin and temptation, not the mere receiving of blessings.[40] Contrary to some popular faith teaching today, Simpson declared, "Faith must always abandon itself before it can claim its blessing."[41] Simpson explained that, like Lot, people with an "earthly spirit" tend to "contend for the best of the land." But, in contrast, faith yields before it can be released: "The man of faith can let the present world go because he knows he has a better, but even as he lets it go God tells him that all things are his because he is Christ's."[42]

Christ-centered faith, Simpson asserted, does not act on human faith or word. He admonished against having faith in your own faith: "Faith is hindered most of all by what we call 'our faith.'"[43] Referring to Mark 11:22–24, he advised, "Jesus does not say to us, 'Have great faith yourselves.' But He does say, 'have the faith of God.'"[44] By this he meant that God imparts a special measure of divine faith to us. Contrary to some modern teachers, Simpson explained, "It is not the faith that heals. God heals, but faith receives it."[45]

## You, Too, Can Exercise Holy, Christ-Centered Faith!

Simpson best expressed this Christ-centered faith in his hymn "Himself." This, too, can be your testimony of faith:

Once it was the blessing, Now it is the Lord;
Once it was the feeling, Now it is His Word;

Once His gifts I wanted, Now the Giver own;
Once I sought for healing, Now Himself alone.

Once 'twas painful trying, Now 'tis perfect trust;
Once a half salvation, Now the uttermost!
Once 'twas ceaseless holding, Now He holds me fast;
Once 'twas constant drifting, Now my anchor's cast.

Once 'twas busy planning, Now 'tis trustful prayer;
Once 'twas anxious caring, Now He has the care;
Once 'twas what I wanted, Now what Jesus says;
Once 'twas constant asking, Now 'tis ceaseless praise.

Once it was my working, His it hence shall be;
Once I tried to use Him, Now He uses me;
Once the power I wanted, Now the Mighty One;
Once for self I labored, Now for Him alone.[46]

## THINK AND DISCUSS

1. What kinds of inheritance can you claim in Christ? What types of inheritance can you not receive in this life?
2. What negative things do you need to avoid? What positive things can you think on, confess and exercise faith for?
3. How can you connect with God?
4. What in your life do you need to be discerning about?
5. Discuss Simpson's principles of healing. When is it appropriate to use and not to use medicine? How much health and healing can we expect in this life? Which of Simpson's healing principles is the most meaningful to you?

6. Describe characteristics of a Christ-centered faith.
7. Which of Simpson's principles of faith is the most helpful to you? Why?

## READ MORE ABOUT IT

### Biographical

A. W. Tozer, *Wingspread* (Camp Hill, Pa.: Christian Publications, 1943)

Robert L. Niklaus, John S. Sawin and Samuel J. Stoesz, *All for Jesus* (Camp Hill, Pa.: Christian Publications, 1986)

### Books by A. B. Simpson

*The Land of Promise* (Harrisburg, Pa.: Christian Publications, 1969)

*The Highest Christian Life* (Harrisburg, Pa.: Christian Publications, 1966)

*A Larger Christian Life* (Camp Hill, Pa.: Christian Publications, 1988)

*Seeing the Invisible* (Camp Hill, Pa.: Christian Publications, 1994)

*The Gospel of Healing* (Harrisburg, Pa.: Christian Publications, 1915)

### Devotional Book by A. B. Simpson

*Days of Heaven on Earth* (Camp Hill, Pa.: Christian Publications, 1984)

# 9

## Oswald Chambers
### (1874–1917)

*His Utmost for God's Highest*

---

**Faith principle:**

*Faith exercises uncommon sense.*

---

Young Oswald Chambers was destined for a great career in the fine arts. He was a talented poet and skilled artist, having studied at prestigious schools of his time. His parents supported his career choice and he had a Christian girlfriend who encouraged him. He was a committed Christian, having been converted through the preaching of Charles Spurgeon. He envisioned using the arts for the glory of God to bring others to Christ and artistic awareness and acceptability to the Church. God had paved the way and provided finances for all his schooling.

There were just two problems. Oswald was going through a dry spell spiritually, and no doors were opening for adequate work. Second, someone had prophesied to him that he was destined to become a minister. It did not make sense to him. He responded that the Lord would have to make it so clear to him that to do anything else would be disobedience.

How did Oswald Chambers solve this dilemma? When things do not make sense, Chambers realized, faith needs to exercise an uncommon sense—what he called "the sense of the Father," a faith that transcends reason and common sense. After hours and days of agonizing prayer he heard an audible voice from God, saying, "I want you in My service—but I can do without you." As he would later advocate again and again to others, he abandoned himself to God—he put himself in God's hands, being willing to do whatever God desired, and trusting God to make a way. He desired to give his utmost for God's highest. As a result, he ended up training to become a minister, giving up his promising career in the arts and eventually his long-time girlfriend.

## Meet Oswald Chambers

When he abandoned himself to God, God did not abandon him. In just a few short years God opened doors for ministry beyond what he could dream. Consider some of the Lord's accomplishments through his life:

- He walked a life of faith like George Müller and Hudson Taylor, and God abundantly provided for all his needs.
- He was launched into a worldwide ministry but retained godly humility.
- He became principal of a Bible training college in England, equipping leaders for ministry.

- He blended intellectual study with strong faith, holiness and practical Christian living.

- He gave up leadership of the Bible training college to serve as a YMCA chaplain in World War I, enhancing and challenging the spiritual lives of hundreds of soldiers and transforming the atmosphere of the British army base in Egypt.

- His devotional work *My Utmost for His Highest*, compiled posthumously by his wife, has become a twentieth-century classic.

- He died at the young age of 43, yet his teachings have had greater impact after his death.

Eugene Peterson describes his impact upon the twentieth century: "So many of us have read his words—been deepened by his prayers, been brought before God by his writing."[1] Another scholar, James Engel, writes, "*My Utmost for His Highest* has become an essential part of the process of maturity for countless Christians over many decades."[2] What made Oswald Chambers the man of faith and godliness through whom countless numbers of people have been blessed? Below are some of the key principles of his walk of faith.

### *Let God Engineer*

This was Oswald Chambers' often-repeated motto. Like a great chess master, God knows the playing board and anticipates the moves of others several moves ahead. He plans His strategy accordingly and engineers circumstances and people to accomplish His sovereign purposes. For example, Chambers was informed that a couple who had been employed for cooking and cleaning for the Bible college under his leadership were pilfering food and dry goods. His response was to pray, trust

God implicitly and wait for Him to move. Eventually the man came to Oswald and confessed. He replied, "I have known all along, but I was waiting for the Holy Spirit to speak to you." As a result, the couple was converted to Christ.[3]

Chambers was dubbed "the apostle of the haphazard" because of his carefree reliance on God to work His will in the haphazard happenings of life. "Be reckless for Jesus Christ," he wrote his wife.[4] When God seemed not to be at work, he called it "God's parenthesis," believing that God had a plan and would bring it about in His way and time.[5] He counseled in such circumstances, "Pay attention to the Source and God will look after the outflow."[6]

Chambers learned and practiced in his own life the maxim from Hudson Taylor: "Have faith in the faithfulness of God, not your own faithfulness." When we try to help God fulfill His purposes for our lives by trusting in ourselves, our ideas and our actions, we actually hinder His working. Chambers writes that if our faith is misplaced, "all our activities are fussy impertinences which tell God He is doing nothing."[7] He advised putting our trust—who we are and what we have—in Christ: "Think of the things you are trying to have faith for! Stop thinking of them and think about your station in God through receiving Christ Jesus."[8]

### Seek the Kingdom of God, Not Prosperity or Success

Since we are heirs with Christ, as Oswald Chambers recognized, should we not seek to possess our inheritance? On the contrary, on the basis of Matthew 6:33, Chambers exhorted, "We are not to seek success or prosperity."[9] Rather, real faith acts by seeking first the Kingdom of God, trusting Him to provide all we need. Chambers grieved over what he called "success-lusting" ministers and Christian workers.[10] Early in his college studies he learned to trust in God for his needs, remarking, "Really God does bless in temporal ways those who put implicit trust in Him."[11] When he made his worldwide journey in 1907 he traveled by faith without income. He remarked that he returned with more money than he had when he left.[12] Chambers testified that whenever he gave sacrificially, God doubled: "The Lord always gives double for all I give away."[13]

He often gave money to poor people without trying to ensure it would not be misused. He reasoned that the Lord commanded to give to all who ask. He believed his responsibility is the giving; God's responsibility is looking after who comes to ask.[14] On one occasion an intoxicated man approached him for a handout. After silently listening to the man, he responded, "Man, I believe your story is all lies, but my Master tells me to give to everyone that asks, so there is my last shilling." After he gave the man the coin he realized it was half a crown, worth two and a half times more, but nonetheless he gave him a blessing. When criticized for his action, he replied that he believed "beggars are sent to test our faith." The next morning he received in the mail a gift from an invalid for three times the amount he had given away the night before.[15]

If we are children of the King in the Kingdom of God, shouldn't we go first class as royalty, rather than deny ourselves? In contrast both to some modern prosperity teachers *and* to their critics, when Oswald Chambers took a voyage he did not travel first or third class, but rather stayed in second-class cabins. On his ship to America, his second-class cabin was described as "not luxurious, but much more comfortable than the crowded compartments below."[16]

Ultimately, he believed that "if you are living the life of faith you will exercise your right to waive your rights, and let God choose for you."[17] He warned against claiming the privileges of the believer solely for one's self:

> If you ask for things from life instead of from God, you ask amiss, i.e., you ask from a desire for self-realization. The more you realize yourself the less you will seek God. . . . The disposition of sin is not immorality and wrongdoing, but the disposition of self-realization—I am my own god. . . . it has the one basis, my claim to my right to myself.[18]

He stressed that exercising faith is not dictating to God. He claimed the promises of God[19] but also warned that believers have a tendency to "tie God up in His own laws and allow Him no free will."[20] In other words, we cannot manipulate God. Chambers suggested that we do a self-inventory of our prayer life and ask the question "Is the Son of God praying in me or am I dictating to Him?"[21]

Chambers waived his rights when he sensed God calling him to serve in the armed forces as a YMCA chaplain in World War I. He could have remained as principal of the Bible training college, for which he had great vision and success. Yet once again he abandoned himself to God, surrendering to His leading for his life, even though it meant less recognition and opportunity for international ministry.

### Exercise Your Faith by Your "Say So"

Like Phoebe Palmer and other evangelical leaders a century ago, Oswald Chambers also advocated positive confession of our faith, citing Romans 10:9–10: "In the Bible confession and testimony are put in a prominent place, and the test of a person's moral character is his 'say so.' I may try and make myself believe a hundred and one things, but it will never be mine until I 'say so.' If I say with myself what I believe and confess it with my mouth, I am lifted into the domain of that thing."[22] Speaking forth what we believe helps to make our faith airborne. At the same time, however, Chambers cautioned that the name of Jesus is not a magic word; it should not be used as a formula or like an incantation.[23] It must be faith imparted by God, not man's faith or his words of faith.

## Avoid Showing Off Your Faith in God's Power

Oswald Chambers believed in the reality of supernatural power from the Holy Spirit, yet he also admonished against becoming preoccupied with it: "Our Lord did not say that signs and wonders would not follow, but that the one set purpose for us is that we do God's will in His way, not our way."[24] He was not opposed to the supernatural gifts, just the misuse and overemphasis of them. He had witnessed the gift of prophecy exercised in his own life, believed that healing was a provision of the atonement of Christ and had personally received revelation from God. Yet he also warned:

> The temptation to the Church is to go into the "show business." . . . It sounds right to ask God to produce signs and wonders, and all through the twenty centuries of the Christian era this temptation has been yielded to, every now and again, in the most wild and inordinate manner. . . . Hundreds of those who were really enlightened by the Spirit of God have gone off on the line of this temptation.[25]

He believed in the reality of supernatural spiritual experiences but cautioned, "Experience is a gateway, not an end. Beware of building your faith on experience."[26]

## *Use Your God-Given Mind along with Your Faith*

Some people believe that education and reason are detriments to strong exercise of faith. They believe that reason or "sense knowledge" and revelation are opposed to each other. While Chambers did acknowledge a difference between such revelation knowledge and sense knowledge, in contrast, he asserted, "Common sense is a gift which God gave to human nature. . . . God instructs us in what we choose, that is, He guides our common sense."[27] Chambers' pet peeve was what he called "intellectual slovenliness." He chided one of his closest friends who asserted that he read only the Bible and books about the Bible:

> You have allowed part of your brain to stagnate for want of use. . . . My strong advice to you is to soak, soak, soak in philosophy and psychology, until you know more of these subjects than ever you need consciously to think. It is ignorance of these subjects on the part of ministers and workers that has brought our evangelical theology to such a sorry plight.
>
> When people refer to a man as "a man of one book," meaning the Bible, he is generally found to be a man of multitudinous books, which simply isolates the one Book to its proper grandeur. The man who reads only the Bible does not, as a rule, know it or human life.[28]

Oswald Chambers was, in reality, an intellectual mystic. That might seem an oxymoron to some; however, Chambers wed together scholarly study with mystical thought and experience. He learned Hebrew, Greek, Latin, French and German as well as organ, piano and art. He studied philosophers like Plato, Socrates, Aristotle and Hegel, and psychological theorists like William James, John Stuart Mill and Herbert Spencer. He drank deeply of poets like Wordsworth, Tennyson and Browning, reformers such as Luther, and Christian mystics such as John of the Cross, John Tauler, Teresa of Avila, Thomas à Kempis, Madame Guyon, François Fénelon and the *Theologia Germanica*.[29] At the same time, he lived a daring walk of faith. While some advocates of faith believe education is where you "get your learnin' and lose your burnin'," Chambers' life demonstrates to us that intellectual study can enhance our faith.

### Exercise Your Faith to Transcend Reason with Uncommon Sense (Revelation)

Though Chambers believed that reason (what he calls "common sense") has a valid and important role in the Christian life, he also cautioned it should be kept in its proper place: "Never enthrone common sense."[30] Having studied the secular philosophers and the Christian mystics, Chambers concluded that faith and revelation transcend common sense. He gave testimony of God's working in his own life that God blessed and made him a blessing to others only as "I am bold enough to trust His leading and not the dictates of my own wisdom and common sense."[31] Common sense is not always the "sense of my Father," because "God is not a fact of common sense, but of revelation."[32] When the Spirit of God was near him, wrote Chambers, "all the lower common-sense things have dwindled away down into their proper proportions."[33] He intimated that he would not have entered the ministry if he had followed common sense, for he was on his way to a great career in the field of art.

Similar to those who differentiate between revelation knowledge and sense knowledge, Oswald Chambers distinguished between "revelation sense" or "revelation facts" and "common sense" or "common-sense facts," when he said, "The Bible does not deal in common-sense facts; the natural universe deals in common-sense facts, and we get at these by our senses. The Bible deals with revelation facts, facts we cannot get at by our common sense, facts we may be pleased to make light of by our common sense."[34] Again he wrote, "Nothing Jesus Christ ever said is common sense, it is revelation sense, and it reaches the shores where common sense fails."[35]

However, Chambers ardently advocated using our powers of reason as long as they are submitted to revelation and faith: "Faith in antagonism to common sense is fanatical, and common sense in antagonism to faith is rationalism. The life of faith brings the two into a right relation."[36] In contrast to some modern faith teaching, Chambers did not set revelation knowledge in opposition to sense knowledge. Instead, he acknowledged that revelation knowledge surpasses sense knowledge, and the two can work hand in hand. Common sense is lower and the leading of the Spirit of God is higher.[37] He advised, "When you are rightly related to God, it is a life of freedom and liberty and delight, you *are* God's will, and all your common-sense decisions are God's will for you unless He checks."[38]

### Let the Written Word Become a Living Word to You

A key to receiving revelation from God is receiving from the Holy Spirit a fresh understanding of Scripture. Oswald Chambers distinguished between the written Word of God and the living Word of God: "The written Word became a Living Word."[39] By this he meant that the living Word, Jesus Christ, causes the written Word to become personally alive to us: "The Scriptures do not give us life unless Jesus speaks them to us."[40] This is similar to the special word from God, or *rhema*, that Spurgeon experienced. Chambers explained how God illuminates a Scripture: "The Holy Spirit exercises a remarkable power in that He will frequently take a text out of its Bible context and put it into the context of our lives. We have all had the experience of a verse coming to us right out of its Bible setting and becoming alive in the settings of our own lives, and that word becomes a sacred, secret possession."[41]

This word, however, is not merely an impulse or impression but rather the convicting and enlightening work of the Spirit. Chambers cautioned:

> The way we are renewed is not by impulses or impressions, but by being gripped by the Word of God. The habit of getting a word from God is right; don't give up till you get one. Never go on an impression, that will pass, there is nothing in it; there is nothing lasting until a word becomes living; when it does it is the Holy Spirit bringing back to your remembrance some word of Jesus Christ.[42]

Further, he admonished, "Beware of impressions and impulses unless they wed themselves to the standards given by Jesus Christ."[43] Thus, an impression or impulse is not to be acted upon unless it is assured to be from Christ or until it is confirmed by a *rhema,* a living word from the Holy Spirit: "No man by mere high human wisdom would dare undertake a step for Jesus' sake unless he knows that the Holy Spirit has directly spoken to him."[44] He learned this principle as a young man when an old praying saint taught him to get "permission of the Holy Ghost" to talk to someone about his spiritual condition.[45] Chambers realized then that he really did not know much about the Holy Spirit and His ways of working.

Chambers came to realize that Jesus Christ Himself is the ultimate living Word, so that our faith ultimately must be in Him, not just in His words. Chambers explained, "Faith is not in what Jesus says, but in Himself; if we only look at what He says we shall never believe."[46] In Galatians 2:20, Chambers discovered that Jesus Christ imparted His own faith to Paul, and he came to the personal realization that "literally, the faith that was in Christ Jesus is now in me."[47] Chambers summarized the position of the classic faith writers: "If we have faith at all, it must be faith in Almighty God."[48]

Once again, referring to Galatians 2:20, Chambers said, "'I live by the faith of the Son of God.' This faith is not Paul's faith in Jesus Christ, but the faith that the Son of God has imparted to him. . . . It is no longer faith in faith."[49] Further he counseled, "Stick steadfastly, not to your faith, but to the one who gives you the faith."[50] In fact, he goes so far as to assert that unless faith is in God alone, it is an illusion.[51]

### When Answers Fail, Look to God for a Deeper Meaning

Perhaps one of the great lessons of faith from Oswald Chambers comes not from his life or his words but rather his death. Have you ever had a time when you thought you had received an assurance or answer to a prayer, or a word from the Lord that did not appear to come true—that seemed to fail? This was the experience of Biddy, the wife of Oswald Chambers.

At the age of 43, in the midst of an energetic schedule and vision for the future, Oswald began experiencing abdominal pain. At first it was diagnosed as a stomach virus, but the pain intensified. Finally going to the hospital, Chambers immediately had surgery for an emergency appendectomy. Initially he seemed to be recovering well, then he suddenly took a serious turn for the worse, hemorrhaging from blood clots in his lungs.

He had been near death but appeared for a while to be improving. Biddy recalled, "Through all the days of the illness and its crises, the word which held me was, 'This sickness is not unto death, but for the glory of God,' and there were times when it seemed that the promise was to have a literal fulfillment. But again God had a fuller meaning."[52]

Why would God allow a great Christian leader to die in the prime of his life and ministry? Some would disparage the thought that Biddy had really heard from the Lord and would claim she was deluded. Others might speculate that Chambers had harbored some secret sin. Still others would avow that there must have been a lack of faith in Biddy or Oswald or their friends.

But all those claims would be false. Ultimately, Biddy received reassurance from the Lord that there was "a fuller meaning." While grieving over his death and asking why it had happened, "the last words she had heard Oswald speak came back to her powerfully in the twilight quiet, 'Greater works than these shall he do, because I go unto my Father.'"[53] She went on to compile his writings into what has become one of the greatest devotional classics, *My Utmost for His Highest,* as well as many of his other teachings.

Yet another close friend who was disheartened by his death experienced a vision of Oswald comforting and encouraging her. The words she heard Chambers speak in the vision were typical of his attitude while living: "Let not your heart be troubled. It's all right; you can't understand God's ways but get down into His love. Don't lose your grip. Be radiant for Him."[54] To all who have experienced deep loss, who have been disillusioned, who have felt like the promises of God have failed, Oswald Chambers would still speak these words of faith today.

## God Can Do Mighty Things through You!

Rev. David Lambert expresses the impact of his life in a memorial tribute, declaring that Chambers' life was

> the finest commentary on the Sermon on the Mount I know. . . . The most precious thing that has come to many of us through the message of God's beloved servant, Oswald Chambers, is that for the lowliest, least promising, and most insignificant person, the Great Life is possible. The mightiest things are made available for ordinary persons in and through Christ Jesus our Lord. God help us to follow him as he followed Christ.[55]

Even if you believe yourself to be the lowliest, least promising and most insignificant person, if you will give your utmost for God's highest like Oswald Chambers, the Great Life is possible for you. God can do mighty things in and through your life of faith in Him.

### THINK AND DISCUSS

1. In what ways can you let God engineer in your life?
2. What does it mean to seek the Kingdom of God? How can you seek first the Kingdom of God?
3. What personal rights do you need to be willing to waive in order to accomplish God's will in your life?
4. Discuss Chambers' statement "Experience is a gateway, not an end. Beware of building your faith on experience." Why does he give this caution?

5. Are faith and reason incompatible? Why or why not? How can faith and reason work together?
6. Describe a time in which a passage of Scripture became alive to you.
7. Have you found a deeper meaning from God in a time when your prayers seemed to be unanswered? Explain how it became meaningful.
8. Which of Oswald Chambers' principles of faith is the most helpful to you and why?

## READ MORE ABOUT IT

### Biographical

Biddy Chambers, ed., *Oswald Chambers: His Life and Work* (London: Simpkin Marshall, 1941)

David McCasland, *Oswald Chambers: Abandoned to God* (Grand Rapids: Discovery House Publishers, 1993)

David W. Lambert, *Oswald Chambers* (Minneapolis: Bethany House, 1997)

### Books by Oswald Chambers

*Biblical Psychology* (Grand Rapids: Discovery House Publishers, 1962, 1995)

*The Place of Help* (Grand Rapids: Discovery House Publishers, 1935, 1989)

*The Psychology of Redemption* (London: Marshall, Morgan, & Scott, 1930, 1963)

### Devotional Books by Oswald Chambers

*Daily Thoughts for Disciples* (Grand Rapids: Discovery House, 1994)

Glenn D. Black, editor, *Devotions for a Deeper Life* (Grand Rapids: Zondervan, 1986)

*My Utmost for His Highest* (New York: Dodd, Mead, 1935, 1965)

*Still Higher for His Highest* (Grand Rapids: Zondervan, 1970)

# 10

## Amy Carmichael
### (1867–1951)
### Model of Selfless Faith

---

**Faith principle:**

*You can hear from God.*

---

After the death of her father, Amy Carmichael found a surrogate father and spiritual mentor in Mr. Wilson, a co-founder of the Keswick deeper Christian life conventions in England. Both his wife and his only daughter, about the age of Amy, had passed away as well. In their loneliness they became very close, and Amy affectionately called him D.O.M. (Dear Old Man). Eventually, she changed her name to Amy Wilson Carmichael. Amy was deeply committed to Jesus Christ and sought to do His will. On January 13, 1892, she received a clear divine impulse, as sure as if it were an audible human voice, "Go ye." She could neither escape nor resist it. It was an undeniable call from God to go into missions.

But how could she leave her D.O.M. now at this point in their lives? He would be crushed at losing another deeply loved one. She felt torn by what she knew unmistakably to be the will of God and her love for her second father, writing, "I feel as though I had been stabbing someone I loved. . . . Through all the keen sharp pain which has come since Wednesday, the certainty that it was His voice I heard has never wavered, though all my heart has shrunk from what it means, though I seem torn in two."[1] The words of Scripture came to her:

> If any man will come after me, let him deny himself, and take up his cross, and follow me. For whosoever will save his life shall lose it: and whosoever will lose his life for my sake shall find it.
>
> Matthew 16:24–25

> He that loveth father or mother more than me is not worthy of me.
>
> Matthew 10:37

> To obey is better than sacrifice. . . .
>
> 1 Samuel 15:22

So she had to go, and made her decision to "trust and obey." But she came under severe criticism. Mr. Wilson's sons thought it was callous and unkind. Others, even leaders, warned her that leaving him would kill him. Her aunts believed she was just captivated with the adventure of going off to a foreign land.

At first she had no idea where she was to go, only that she had been called to go. Bit by bit, step by step God revealed to her through Scripture, impressions from Him, and circumstances what she was to do and where she was to go. She finally believed that she was to join the China Inland Mission, so she made preparations and packed her bags. At the last minute the mission doctor would not release her to go to China.

Mr. Wilson responded ecstatically, "God has given me back my Isaac!" However, it was not to be for long. The burden still weighed upon Amy's heart, and she continued seeking God. One year later, to the day, she heard "Go ye," and had a strong urging, an unusual sense, that she was to go to Japan. She struggled through her feelings of leaving once again. Nonetheless, this time the doors opened, and in less than two months she was sailing to Japan.[2]

This was just the beginning of an incredible missionary career of faith spanning nearly sixty years in Japan, China, Ceylon and finally India (where she spent 53 years without a furlough). She was perhaps one of the most selfless, giving persons of the twentieth century—an example of a faith unconcerned about self.

## Meet Amy Carmichael

Raised as an Irish Presbyterian, Amy Carmichael was a friend of Hudson Taylor's daughter-in-law. Her ministry was influenced heavily by his faith principles of trusting God for provision of needs. She became a skilled writer and poet. She was also involved in the Keswick Holiness movement, contributing frequently to its magazine *The Life of Faith*. Practicing the faith of Müller and Taylor, she took her needs to God, not men.

Her acts of faith included the following:

- Like George Müller, Amy made specific requests to God and believed for specific amounts. And God provided just as she requested.

- Amy came to believe in the power of God according to Mark 16:17–18, and operated in gifts of healing, casting out demons, receiving prophetic words from the Lord, prophetic dreams and visions, miraculous provision and protection, extraordinary answers to prayer and other supernatural encounters.[3]
- When cholera struck the village of Dohnavur, it infested people all around them but never invaded the mission compound.
- Amy founded Dohnavur Fellowship to rescue young girls from Hindu temple prostitution.
- She boldly walked into forbidden places and was protected by the Lord.

Amy Carmichael yearned for more of the supernatural power of God, of which Hudson Taylor spoke, saying, "I don't wonder apostolic miracles have died. Apostolic living certainly has."[4] Her life demonstrates one who lived with apostolic power and heard from the Lord.

How do we hear the voice of God? How do we know the impulses we receive are divinely impressed upon us? The life and message of Amy Carmichael shows us the following keys to divine guidance in the walk of faith.

### Be Still and Know

Amy Carmichael had come under criticism for taking off to Japan for a missions venture. She knew clearly from the Lord that she had been called, yet even some of her friends questioned her call. She realized she had made mistakes in implementing that call, some due to fear, and came to realize that there is a time to act and a time to wait in working out the call of God. She confessed, "So I tried and we tried—and failed. He had to teach us to Be Still and Know. Then when His time came His will was clear."[5] Through the experiences of her life she learned the secret of waiting on the Lord: "I cannot fly in spirit ('mount up with wings as eagles'), I cannot 'run, and not be weary,' I cannot 'walk, and not faint,' till my will is content with God's will."[6]

On one occasion, when other missionaries were on furlough, she was burdened with the responsibility of the work of the mission. As she quieted her heart and mind before the Lord she received a vision of Jesus in the garden of the compound, which encouraged her. He was kneeling under the tamarind trees surrounding the mission cottage (which in the vision changed to olive trees) and was praying for the children. She then realized it was not her work, but His. The weight was on His shoulders, not hers. She was encouraged and her attitude changed. She felt compelled to kneel in the garden beside Him to share the burden, realizing that it was the only fitting response.[7]

It takes faith just to be still and wait on the Lord. Amy found in her own life:

> If I cannot catch "the sound of the noise of rain" long before the rain falls, and, going to some hilltop of the spirit, as near to my God as I can, have not faith to wait there with my face between my knees, though six times or sixty times I am told "there is nothing," till at last "there arises a little cloud out of the sea," then I know nothing of Calvary love. . . .[8]

### Desire God, Not Worldly Desires, and He Will Guide Your Desires

Psalm 37:4 counsels us, "Delight yourself in the LORD and he will give you the desires of your heart" (NIV). Some people put the proverbial cart before the horse, and with mixed motives declare, "I will delight myself in the Lord, so that I can get my desires." Amy Carmichael cautioned against trusting our own desires: "God has something much better for us than the thing we naturally desire. As we wait with all the desire of our mind fixed on Him, the thing we naturally long for becomes less pressing, the friction ceases, and we are set free to go on."[9] When we truly delight in the Lord we want what He wants, not what we want. He changes and conforms our desires into His desires.

It is not that God is a killjoy and does not want us to be happy, but rather God knows what is best for us. And we are willing to give up anything we desire, anything we treasure for His sake. Amy explains:

> Those of us who are God's emissaries are to treat the world (not just its corruptions, but its legitimate joys, its privileges and blessings also), as a thing to be touched at a distance. . . . It is not that He forbids us this or that indulgence or comfort. . . . No, it is that we who love our Lord, and we whose affections are set on the things that are heaven for us today—we voluntarily and gladly lay aside things that charm the world, so that we may be charmed and ravished by the things of heaven. . . . to look upon the world, in all its delights and attractions, suspecting that traps are set there for us, reserving ourselves for a higher way. *The world is not for us.*[10]

Some today teach that because we are "King's Kids," children of the King of kings, God wants us always to go first class and have the very best of everything. Amy Carmichael counseled otherwise, saying she believed that Jesus and His disciples would not travel first class, that "this missionary habit of going by the easier rather than the harder way, when He chose the harder" does not bring glory to the Lord. Rather, "it is as if we put ourselves a little above Him."[11] It is, instead, a matter of attitude and humility. When asked why she went third class when traveling on a ship, her reply was, "Because there is no fourth class."[12] She opposed what she called "fashionable Christianity,"[13] in contrast to some today who would claim riches as the privilege of being a child of the King. Amy's life modeled selflessness, for she gave up all rights to herself.

Yet, we might ask, is it always inappropriate to go first class or desire the finest? There were rare occasions in which Amy Carmichael did disregard her own standard. She would travel first class on a ship if she was not feeling well, or to obtain adequate sleep, sanitation and undisturbed solitude. On certain occasions she was also willing to "go first class" for building projects. She understood that it could be proper to use God's money for more costly supplies if finances were given expressly for that function. In those cases, she accepted it as divine permission. She would pray and believe for abundance. She received insight from the Lord regarding the feeding of the five thousand, that just as after giving and giving, the disciples still had enough left over for their needs, so according to her faith, the Lord promised her, "there should be baskets over and above our daily supplies."[14] Ultimately, Amy showed us that the supreme motive for our desires must be selfless love:

> If I hold on to choices of any kind, just because they are my choice; if I give any private room to my likes and dislikes, then I know nothing of Calvary love.
>
> If I put my own happiness before the well being of the work entrusted to me; if, though I have this ministry and have received much mercy, I faint, then I know nothing of Calvary love. . . .[15]

### You Can Receive a Word from the Lord

Amy frequently received clear direction from the Lord: "Do this. Go there." She had heard what seemed almost an audible voice saying, "Go ye," bidding her to go to the mission field. Later, the direction became more specific: "Go to Japan." Later, while in Japan, the unmistakable call came again, this time to go to Ceylon.[16] She received what she called "shewings," insights obtained in a unique manner from the Holy Spirit.[17] She remarked, "One *dare* not do anything but obey when that Voice speaks."[18] How did she know that she was hearing from God? There were three ways she received her leadings.

### THROUGH THE WORD OF GOD

It would come to her clearly with an "unanswerable force."[19] One manner was through a distinctive energizing of Scripture in what she called a *durbar,* an Indian term for an exceptionally privileged audience with a high-ranking leader, which she associated with the Hebrew word *dabar,* "to speak a word":

> When reading your Bible, have you not often noticed that some word has shone out in a new, direct, clear way to you? It has been as though you have never read it before. You cannot explain the vivid freshness, the life, in it, the extraordinary way it has leapt to your eye—to your heart. It just was so. That was the "durbar"; you were in the very presence of your King at that moment. He was speaking to you. His word was spirit and life.[20]

This is, as we have seen in earlier chapters, what is sometimes called today a *rhema,* a special personal word from God.

### THROUGH CIRCUMSTANCES

Circumstances are not always an indication from God but often can be ordered by God as a confirming witness. She would review and analyze the circumstances—how the decision would affect others, resources and help available, people she had met as divine encounters. Sometimes God leads, Amy discovered, through the little, imperceptible circumstances of life. Sometimes, she realized, it is just a matter of faithful perseverance, of keeping on.

Amy also recognized, like Oswald Chambers, that God sometimes engineers circumstances, maneuvering people and situations to meet His purposes. She prayed to meet Raj, a notorious outlaw and leader of a ring of bandits, so that she might witness to him. One day in a field three armed men carrying weapons strode out from behind some rocks as if to attack her. The leader of the band was Raj! Unruffled, she invited them to sit down and have tea and bread with her, and they complied. He eventually gave his life to Christ. Later, when he was in prison falsely accused and blackmailed, Amy dreamed that the gates of the prison would open on their own as in Acts 12. When she went to the prison to visit him, the gates opened automatically just as she had dreamed and she walked right into the quarters. Convinced of Raj's sincere faith and awed by the opening of the gates, a friend of Amy's who was a bishop consented to baptize him.[21]

## THROUGH THE INWARD LEADING OF THE HOLY SPIRIT

Like Spurgeon, Amy Carmichael believed in receiving a "word from the Lord": "This 'word' might be something remembered at the crucial moment, or a direct command."[22] When she lacked inner peace or an open door, she asked for a sign, which the Lord almost invariably gave to her. She frequently received clear words that "cannot be mistaken."[23]

Sometimes Amy was led within her spirit by an "irresistible divine pressure."[24] While in Japan she felt "pressed in spirit" to ask in prayer for one soul, one person to receive Christ as Savior. The next day a young silk weaver became a Christian. A month later she felt strongly impressed to ask for two souls. And, indeed, two more people came to the Lord shortly thereafter. Two weeks later she received the divine urging again, this time to pray for four souls "to cross the line" into faith. Some of the missionaries joined with her in believing for four people to be saved, but others thought it was presumptuous to expect such quick results, especially if, as Amy argued, they should go against Chinese customs and ask converts to burn their idols. Amazingly, four people came to salvation the very next day. Several weeks later, once again, she sensed the divine compulsion, this time to pray for eight conversions in another location. Once again she received resistance from several Christians there. Finally, the leader of the group, an older, cautious man, yielded to Amy, saying, "You are a Jesus-walking one; if His voice speaks to you, although it speaks not to us, we will believe." And, yes, eight people quickly received Jesus Christ![25]

It is important to note that Amy did not claim specific numbers of people in faith on her own accord but only when specially led of the Lord to do so. Like George Müller, she sought the Lord for His will, and then, under divine impulse or burden placed on her by the Lord, made her request to Him. For example, she did not go on to claim sixteen on the next missions visit. In fact, she received no divine impression to pray for a certain number of people to be saved. Some did indeed come to Christ, but she took no tally of how many.

Amy also experienced supernatural visions and dreams from time to time. Even when she did experience such a phenomenon, she did not automatically accept it as from the Lord but tested it by the three means mentioned above. She would ask herself whether it really came from

God or was a false impression. Then she would wait on the Lord and receive further confirmation through a Scripture, circumstances or that inner divine witness of the Spirit.

On one occasion she had a vivid dream of two godly men, one a medical doctor, coming to join her work. She had so much wanted them to come that she struggled with the possibility that her own wishful thinking might have brought on the vision. She stilled her heart before the Lord but heard nothing. God was silent, too. Or so it seemed. Unknown to Amy, however, one man was already on a ship on his way to India. The other man would come months later. To Amy, such times she wrote seemed like an "age-long minute,"[26] but she learned to trust and wait.[27] We can learn from Amy Carmichael to rest and know that God has all things under control.

Amy did not get puffed up about her revelations but humbly acknowledged that God had in His graciousness given light: "If when I am able to discover something which has baffled others, I forget Him who reveals the deep and secret things, and knows what is in the darkness and shows it to us; if I forget that it was He who granted that ray of light to His most unworthy servant, then I know nothing of Calvary love."[28]

### God Turns Our Missteps into His Steps

Amy admitted that sometimes she missed it in hearing from the Lord. When she left for Japan, along the journey she became sick with a high fever and felt very alone. She had many second thoughts and questioned what the will of God really was. She wrote that she was braced for misunderstanding or criticism. She recognized she might be making some mistakes but felt impelled by God just the same.

There were times when she knew she had heard from the Lord but had missed His timing or the way or means He wanted to accomplish His will. Even in those times she sought the Lord and received assurance that He would use even her mistakes to bring about His good. She commented, "All life's training is just exactly what is needed for the true Life-work, still out of view, but far away from none of us. Don't grudge me the learning of a new lesson."[29] She had many "what-ifs" but years later would remember only God's faithfulness in the situation.

Amy could sometimes be demanding and difficult to work for, convinced that her ways were the Lord's ways. Her standards for Dohnavur Fellowship were strict, and many could not endure her ways of living out the life of the cross. Yet she agonized over those who left and those she felt she had to dismiss. Sometimes she wondered how she missed the Lord in bringing them on board into the mission.

Amy compared hearing from God with a shortwave radio. If you are not tuned in precisely, you cannot hear clearly. Or if you do not have the right wavelength, you cannot hear at all. Referring to Westcott's comment on John 12:28–29, she believed that understanding the voice of the Lord hinges on our ability to listen carefully.[30] When she had doubts about the rightness of her decisions, it would send her back to waiting on the Lord and seeking His face: "There is a place where the human fails, breaks down, turns to ashes. Hope has not a single foothold. In such an hour there is a perishing of everything unless the soul waits in silence for God only."[31]

### In Trial, Pain and Loss God Is Still at Work

Her motto was "To will what God wills brings peace."[32] Many times the children she cared for died, in spite of all her healing successes. She remarked that so often soon after a rescued child arrived at the mission

> something almost inevitable happens, sometimes an accident, sometimes an illness. Often, so often, the newly ransomed little one is snatched away by death. It cannot be a mere chance happening. It occurs too frequently for us to think so now. But if the devil has anything to do with it, thank God—after that there is no more that he can do, and his worst only sends the little life far out of his reach forever. It is a mystery, a secret thing, and the secret things belong to the Lord.[33]

She understood that faith will not remove all the puzzles and uncertainties, but faith realizes that the answers are found in God's sovereign purposes.[34]

Within one week death came to one of the dear children, named Lulla, and also to one of the best leaders of her mission, Thomas Walker, who was considered a father and brother to everyone. People around Amy tried to console her even as they acknowledged that it was difficult to imagine how all this could work out for the best. Amy replied, "We are not asked to *see*. Why need we when we *know?*"[35] She knew, according to Romans 8:28, that God causes all things to work together for the best. Amy's attitude reminds me of the words of one of my mentors, "Maturity is to understand that you don't have to understand." Job never received answers from God to all the questions he posed about his sufferings. Yet he came to understand that God is greater.

Amy especially learned this when she fell into a hole and sustained a chronic injury. She believed in healing and did experience brief times of relief, but the pain returned and worsened. She had prayed for others who then received healing; it would not come for her. Yet she had confidence in God, saying, "Faith never wonders why."[36] She believed pain was from the enemy and maintained peace in perseverance, explaining, "So though through these months acceptance has been a word of liberty and victory and peace to me, it has never meant acquiescence in illness, as though ill-health were from Him who delights to deck His priests with health. But it did mean contentment with the unexplained."[37]

Amy viewed her work as being a soldier in the army of the Lord. Wounds and scars are a part of the territory as a soldier, Amy avowed. If you have no wounds or scars, there is a serious question whether you have really served God.[38] The trials of life, to Amy, are God's way of "forging the blade" in the fire to become a tempered instrument of God's warfare. Surviving on the spiritual battlefield of life requires enduring faith.

### Great Faith Demonstrates Faithfulness

Maybe you think you are getting nowhere in life. Maybe you wonder if God is really with you or whether your efforts are worth it. Amy Carmichael's life can encourage you that whatever you do for Jesus, no matter how small and seemingly insignificant, can make a difference. Other missionaries told her that what she was trying to accomplish in rescuing children was just a drop of water in the ocean. She could not possibly hope to change Indian customs and society. She would rescue children, but they would return to their old ways. Or the law stipulated they had to be returned. Or they were threatened. Many of them died.

Yet she stressed faithfulness in the little things: "A little thing is a little thing, but faithfulness in little things is a very great thing."[39] There was nothing too menial or insignificant for her and her co-workers to do. Every child was a soul God loves. Every attempt to change society was a dent in the caste structure.

It is often during a time of waiting, of seemingly just treading water, that God is silently, imperceptibly at work, molding and forging us as His instruments. One British candidate for the ministry became frustrated and impatient that it was taking so long for her to go through the preparation to be released for missions in India. Amy wrote to her, "Think of these two or three years as given to forging the blade for what only a blade of that temper can do."[40] It may be a time of growing, stretching, squeezing, pruning and purging, but God is forming us into the men and women of God He can use best.

Through her faithfulness in reaching out and caring, rescuing one by one, Amy eventually became known and respected throughout India. After several years of ministry in India the governor of Madras sent her an announcement that she was to be awarded a medal for her service and registered with the Royal Birthday Honors List. Yet in her own self-effacing way she questioned why she should receive a medal for serving her Savior, who had been rejected and despised and had died for her. Finally convinced that it would be discourteous to decline the honor, she nonetheless would not attend the award ceremony.[41] Amy's example shows us that everything we do for Jesus can make a difference if we just trust and obey.

### Faith Is Expressed through Calvary Love— A Chance to Die to Self and the World

Amy told of another story, not unlike the martyrdom of the early Church Father Polycarp.[42] Her friend Raj was once again falsely accused and framed, and was surrounded by the police. He threw away his gun (which he had for protection) and shouted to the police, "You whose duty it is to shoot, shoot here," pointing at his heart. The police shot but did not hit him even though the bullets fell all around him. They wondered if he was charmed. He backed up against a large tamarind tree, and they fired again—sixteen bullets. The bullets hit the branches above him, the bark beside him, and the sand in front of him, but not one hit Raj! Then, as he kneeled before them, they grabbed him, one man breaking his arm, another biting him on the neck to "taste the blood from such a man." Finally, they shot him in the head at point-blank range. The one thing Amy had asked of him was that he die without a weapon in his hand. And that he did. He died clean—that was the important thing.[43]

That is the message of Amy Carmichael's walk of faith—Calvary love—to die clean, whether a death to self, to the world or to life itself—to die as Jesus would have us die. The crowning work of Amy Carmichael was her classic little book *If*. It epitomizes her Christian walk and challenges us also to walk in Calvary love—the way of the cross—dying to ourselves and to the world. Financial hardships, loss of those she loved, criticism—all these she viewed as opportunities to die to herself and walk in Calvary love. She expresses it poignantly in *If*:

> If I have not compassion on my fellow-servant even as my Lord had pity on me, then I know nothing of Calvary love. . . .
>
> If I do not feel far more for the grieved Savior than for my worried self when troublesome things occur, then I know nothing of Calvary love. . . .
>
> If I am perturbed by the reproach and misunderstanding that may follow action taken for the good of souls for whom I must give account; if I cannot commit the matter and go on in peace and in silence, then I know nothing of Calvary love. . . .

If my attitude be one of fear, not faith, about one who has disappointed me, if I say, "Just what I expected," if a fall occurs, then I know nothing of Calvary love.[44]

## You, Too, Can Exercise Selfless Faith!

This is the selfless faith Amy Carmichael models for us today. When you seek God's will from your heart He will stir in you all the faith and love you need. The prophetic word from the Lord given to Amy is just as timeless and timely today: "Trust me, My child. Trust Me with a humbler heart and a fuller abandon to My will than ever thou didst before. Trust Me to pour My love through thee. . . ."[45]

## THINK AND DISCUSS

1. What does it mean to wait on the Lord? In what ways can you wait on the Lord? Get alone and spend some time being still before God and listening for His voice.
2. What are some of the things God desires for us? How do they differ from worldly desires?
3. Have you ever received a word from the Lord? Describe it. How did you know that it was from the Lord?
4. How does God turn our missteps into His steps? Describe a time in which you made a mistake but God turned it around for good.
5. In what ways can you practice faithfulness in the little things?
6. How can you demonstrate Calvary love and selfless faith?

7. Which of Amy Carmichael's principles of faith is the most helpful to you and why?

## READ MORE ABOUT IT

### Biographical

Elisabeth Elliot, *A Chance to Die: The Life and Legacy of Amy Carmichael* (Old Tappan, N.J.: Fleming H. Revell, 1987)

### Book by Amy Carmichael

*If* (Grand Rapids: Zondervan, 1980)

### Devotional Books by Amy Carmichael

*Rose from Brier* (Fort Washington, Pa.: Christian Literature Crusade, 1933, 1971)
*Thou Givest . . . They Gather* (Fort Washington, Pa.: Christian Literature Crusade, 1958)

# 11

## John A. MacMillan
### (1873–1956)

### *A Believer with Authority*

---

**Faith principle:**

*You can exercise spiritual authority as a believer.*

---

In Nyack, New York, at the age of 78, John MacMillan, with the aid of others, engaged in intensive multiple deliverance sessions over a three-month period, expelling 171 demons from a young woman. The woman had become infested by the dark powers through living with an aunt who had practiced spiritualism. The spirits manifested violently, trying to harm her or others. Procuring her freedom entailed a long and arduous process, but step by step, through the name and blood of Jesus, she gained victory.

On one occasion when he walked into the room an evil spirit manifested, addressing MacMillan in a male voice through the woman's lips, "I know you from the

Philippines." The demon recognized MacMillan from an encounter about 25 years earlier, thousands of miles away on the other side of the globe. Evidently, MacMillan had gained a reputation in the spirit world for his exercise of spiritual authority. On this occasion, in his characteristically quiet manner, he commanded the spirit to be silent, and in the name of Jesus expelled it from the woman immediately.[1]

## Meet John MacMillan

Who is this man, John MacMillan, and how did he exercise such authority? A meek and quiet Canadian businessman and Presbyterian elder, John MacMillan had a heart for missions. His wife, Isabel, had served as missionary with the China Inland Mission and personal nurse to Hudson Taylor. In 1923, at the age of 49, MacMillan sold his printing business and sailed with his wife and seven-year-old son for China as a missionary with The Christian and Missionary Alliance, later becoming an editor and professor. During the next thirty years he became heavily involved in spiritual warfare, discovering through Scripture and experience that believers can exercise authority over the powers of darkness. These demonstrations of the authority of Christ in MacMillan's ministry included the following:

- *Immobilizing demonic manifestations through power encounters:*

One time a spiritist witchdoctor was performing a ceremony, chanting in a trance-like state and calling on the spirits. A drum in the room began to beat in rhythm without anyone touching it. Then it rose to the ceiling in a state of levitation. MacMillan walked into the room, and took authority over the spirits, rebuking them in the name of Jesus Christ. The drum immediately dropped to the floor and ceased pounding.[2]

• *Claiming divine protection:*

In 1924 an Asiatic strain of cholera spread into an epidemic in the city all around the compound, endangering the mission in South China. MacMillan confessed the Scripture "For he will deliver you from the snare of the fowler and from the deadly pestilence" (Psalm 91:3, RSV). In the following weeks some members of the mission experienced physical weakness and depression, but they came through safely without contagion from the plague.[3]

• *Experiencing remarkable healings:*

Once on an emergency mission trip where he was alone on the rainy slippery trail, MacMillan slipped and broke his ankle. . . . His only recourse was the Lord since he was alone and about twenty miles from even a first aid station. In simple faith, he stepped out and began walking those many miles. He got home safely, and shortly thereafter had the ankle X-rayed. There had been a clean break, but it was perfectly healed.[4]

• *Exercising the authority of binding and loosing:*

In 1924 pirates kidnapped four missionaries in South China. MacMillan and the remaining missionaries joined together in concerted prayer, binding the spirits of evil that incited the kidnappers and declaring the captives loosed. Within days the bandits released two of the missionaries. Another missionary escaped his captors two weeks later. A month after the ordeal began, one man remained captive. After a period of concentrated prayer, with confidence MacMillan declared him loosed in the name of Jesus. The outlaws released him that very day.[5]

- *Turning around a demoralized mission and stirring revival:*

Discouragement and discord plagued the missionaries in the Philippines, and the mission teetered on the verge of closing. In 1926 MacMillan was assigned to head the mission and reverse the tide. Exercising spiritual authority, he bound the spirits of dissension and depression and brought about unity, revitalization, boldness—and a mighty revival in four years, even in the midst of his wife's death.[6]

- *Claiming divine vindication for injustice:*

When MacMillan left to go to the mission field Cross Products contracted to take over mortgage payments on MacMillan's business, and to earmark part of the earnings of the business for MacMillan's family and financial affairs in Toronto, as well as financial support for their mission. About a year after MacMillan arrived in China, Cross broke the contract, putting him thousands of dollars in debt. Praying and believing for a resolution to the injustice, MacMillan spoke with authority, prophesying, "Vengeance is mine, saith the LORD." Persisting in prayer for three years, he received a letter informing him that all back debts had been completely paid off. Cross later attempted a lawsuit against him, but it was blocked. In due course his business went bankrupt, and he reaped the judgment of God for his dishonesty and breach of contract.[7]

- *Authoring the original book on the believer's authority:*

In 1932 John MacMillan wrote a series of articles entitled "The Authority of the Believer," based on Scripture and his experiences of spiritual warfare. Republished as a book with additional teachings, it became popular in evangelical circles throughout the twentieth century.[8] The charismatic and Word of Faith movements have also modified and popularized his concepts.

How did such a gentle and unassuming layman—a Presbyterian no less!—exercise such dynamic authority and power? Through recognizing that every believer has authority in Christ over the powers of evil.

## You Have Scripture-Based Authority as a Child of God

MacMillan advanced the idea that Christians can claim "in prayer the power of the Ascended Lord, and the believer's throne union with Him. . . ."[9] Where in faith the obedient saint claims his throne-rights in Christ, and boldly asserts his authority, the powers of the air will recognize and obey."[10] He believed the rod of Moses

> symbolizes the authority of God committed to human hands. By it the holder is made a co-ruler with his Lord, sharing His throne-power and reigning with Him. . . .
> So today, every consecrated hand that lifts the rod of the authority of the Lord against the unseen powers of darkness is directing the throne-power of Christ against Satan and his hosts in a battle that will last until "the going down of the sun."[11]

He cited several principles for professing the believer's authority, based on our covenant with God:

- *You are a spiritual Israelite and thus inherit the authority and glory of Israel* (see Romans 2:28–29).

191

- *You are a child of the King* (see John 1:12) and should behave appropriately: "We are members of a kingly family, and in our walk and conversation there will be, if we live much in the King's presence, that true courtliness which becomes His children." These he calls "family privileges."[12] That means that you are a prince or a princess, a royal child.

- *You can dwell under the shadow of the Almighty* (see Psalm 91:1):

  > In this supreme ministry of the son of God for lost men there was secured for those who believe Him and abide in Him a sharing in the fulness which He received as Son of man (Col. 2:9), and which makes them partakers of His authority and sharers in His kingdom. Before such overcomers the hosts of hell give way, and the utmost energy of the unseen world cannot harm them as they dwell "in the secret place of the Most High," and "abide under the shadow of the Almighty." . . . In the case of every obedient believer who today fulfils the conditions, God stands waiting to show him His victory.[13]

- *All things are under the feet of Christ and thus also the Church as His Body* (see Ephesians 1:20–23): "'[He] hath put all things under his feet.' The feet are members of the Body. How wonderful to think that the least and lowest members of the Body of the Lord, those who in a sense are the very soles of the feet, are far above all the mighty forces."[14]

- *The Church is seated in the heavenly places in Christ* (see Ephesians 2:6), and therefore shares the throne with Christ as a co-heir (what he and other evangelical leaders call "throne power").

## You Can Claim Divine Protection According to Psalm 91

When MacMillan's son Buchanan was a toddler, he received an emergency call at his printing establishment that the house adjacent to his was ablaze. Unruffled, "he committed the crisis to God in prayer, claiming God's protection according to Psalm 91:10 that 'no destruction would befall the house.'" Hurrying home he arrived to discover that the fire had amazingly halted at a wood fence between the homes, even though the houses were quite close to each other.[15] Later he testified:

> True it is that the angel of the Lord encamps round about them that fear Him, with a view to their deliverance. But the child of God is personally responsible for the definite claiming of such protection, and also for abiding within the circumscribed limits wherein it is effective.
>
> Faith is the channel along which the grace of God flows, consequently, there is the necessity for maintaining a constantly victorious spirit over all the wiles and the attacks of the enemy. . . . More and more, therefore, it is vital that every true servant of God learn the secret of dwelling "in the secret place of the Most High," thereby in all the going out and coming of life, experiencing the security of those who "abide under the shadow of Shaddai."[16]

On another occasion in the Philippines a torrential downpour inundated the mission compound. As MacMillan returned to the property after a Sunday service he was reflecting on dying to self and thus living in Christ. He commented to himself, "I do 'reign with Him.' If the enemy suddenly assails the citadel, he cannot enter, so why should I fear his shouting outside?" At that very moment a tall tree collapsed toward him. MacMillan recounted, "It was graciously guided of God, so that, although the space was comparatively narrow, it fell without damaging the chapel or house, apart from destroying the covering of the stairway to the upstairs door." In this surprising incident of divine intervention Mac-Millan sensed God was giving him a meaningful insight: "The way out is blocked—is it not a gracious call to prayer, lest the great adversary block our efforts and shut us up in a small place? We have prayed for the binding of the strongman—we must watch and pray that the strong man does not bind us."[17]

### You Have Covenant Right to Claim Salvation for Your Family

Do you have a child or close relative who is not a believer or who is living in sin? MacMillan offers you hope. As with the Covenant Theology of Spurgeon, Murray and Simpson, MacMillan believed that as a Christian, you can claim your family for God as a covenant privilege based on Acts 16:31, "Believe in the Lord Jesus, and you will be saved, you and your household" (NASB). However, we cannot presume that salvation of our family is guaranteed, for "salvation is not hereditary, but the covenant of grace provides for the salvation of the children of believers. The believer must claim the covenant and abide in it; and when he does so, its working will be found to be effectual."[18] If you have children who are in rebellion or not walking close to God, MacMillan would counsel you to persevere in your prayers and believe that God will break through in their lives and bring them back to Him.

### You Have Authority over the Devil's Harassments and Oppression

MacMillan realized that the evil forces of Satan often accuse and harass believers. But he also affirmed that we have authority over those dark powers to overcome those attacks on our lives. Some of the areas in which we can exercise spiritual authority include the following:

### AUTHORITY OVER DEPRESSION

MacMillan was convinced from experience that depression often (though not always) comes as an assault from the devil. He endured many such attacks, especially during his ministry in China. Nonetheless, he continued to give thanks to God for victory, even when it was not evident. When attacked by depression he encouraged himself to prevail with "a more positive attitude of resistance."[19] He related an incident during his ministry there:

> A young missionary lady in China, living with two companions in a river port, was suddenly seized with intense depression. So great was the effect upon her that the older missionary in charge sent word to the field chairman that she must be removed as she was causing harm at the station. Accordingly she was sent to the headquarters, where much prayer was offered for her without result, save that her depression seemed to increase.

MacMillan, however, spoke unsympathetically to her, saying, "Miss —, you are doing wrong in keeping up this continued blueness of spirit; I want to tell you that this depression is of the devil." This stunned her because all the other missionaries had tried to comfort her. She became indignant, which MacMillan discerned as "a most hopeful sign." MacMillan restated his counsel, explaining "that the Lord commands all of His followers to rejoice in Him; something she was disobeying." Then he clarified that her condition resulted from "her yielding to the lies of the enemy, and that she must resist the devil." She quickly recovered and returned to her station, "equipped this time to discern the attacks of the devil and to throw them off."[20]

### AUTHORITY OVER UNCONTROLLED ANGER

From his experiences in ministry MacMillan understood that "there is an intimate connection between sinful anger and the prince of evil, and sustained wrath will surely open the door to his entrance." One day MacMillan overheard two native Christian workers, a husband and wife, arguing loudly with each other. John and Isabel quietly but firmly took authority in the name of Jesus over the evil spirits behind the anger, commanding them to leave the couple. "Almost immediately," MacMillan remarked, "the quarreling stopped. As the authority was day by day held and renewed, the spirits were kept in check. Eventually however, the two separated, for they did not seek victory for themselves."[21]

One of the students in the Filipino Bible school displayed a fierce temper. "Stirred up by a trivial matter, he utterly lost control of himself, and speedily became almost insane with rage." MacMillan, as the headmaster, prayed in the adjoining room, taking authority over the spirits of anger in the name of Jesus. In just a few minutes the boy settled down and the demonic forces that had incited him were overcome.[22]

### AUTHORITY OVER EXCESSIVE FEAR

When MacMillan was sailing in a Filipino boat off the coast of Mindanao in the Philippines, sizeable waves arose. His son Buchanan, who usually enjoyed sailing, was suddenly overcome with an uncontrollable fear that he had never had before in rough waters:

He begged to be taken ashore; and as the whole affair seemed to be directed against the progress of the evangelistic trip, [MacMillan] quietly took the authority of Christ over the spirits of fear and rebuked them, though saying nothing openly. In a very few minutes the lad seemed to change completely, and for the remainder of the journey, lasting several days, there was no further difficulty. The second night after, while in the center of a wide bay, and about twelve miles from shore, a heavy squall was encountered, and an outrigger broke. The danger was imminent, but, though the lad was fully aware of it, and though the waves were washing quite over the boat, he manifested not the slightest shrinking.[23]

MacMillan witnessed "other instances of fear, involving older and experienced missionaries," and again rebuked spirits of fear in Jesus' name, resulting in dramatic changes.[24]

### AUTHORITY OVER ADDICTIONS

God manifested amazing power through MacMillan by liberating people from compulsive cravings. A teacher at the boys' school caught a student chewing tobacco and took him to MacMillan. The boy admitted, "I cannot give it up, sir; I have tried again and again, and have failed."

MacMillan replied, "Do you really desire to do so? The Lord Jesus is able to give you grace for victory." After giving him additional instructions, MacMillan interceded for him in prayer, and the young pupil "himself then took hold simply of the Lord."

Several weeks later MacMillan met the boy again and asked, "Are you having victory over the tobacco?"

He replied, "I have not had a single taste for the tobacco since the day we prayed together in your office."

MacMillan recounted the power of God's working: "Thus God, in lands where the weed has been so widespread that practically everyone has used it, is Himself purifying and blessing the lives and bodies of His saved ones."[25]

### AUTHORITY TO OPEN BARRED GATEWAYS TO EVANGELISM AND MISSIONS

As a result of his encounters in China and the Philippines MacMillan discerned that the forces of evil frequently hamper the progress of the Gospel and must be rebuked:

> The enemy has been preternaturally active; he has shut the doors of the lands against the Church's efforts; he presses on her heels as she goes forward. It is a time for those, who know the experience of sitting in heavenly places with the risen Lord, to hold the rod of His authority over the blocked roads before His people that all hindrances may be removed, that the way to the last tribes may be opened and the last individuals of the people for His name may be called out.[26]

Concerning demonic interference with his mission work in the Philippines, MacMillan explained:

> Here are hindrances to advance in the field work. . . . Ignorance binds the heathen mind in darkness that seems impenetrable. . . . Dissensions rise in the ranks of brethren, and the Spirit of peace withdraws. Behind every such situation the presence of the same malign powers can be assumed. The solution is in their displacement—we alone are to blame that they continue in power.
>
> The same principle is often applicable in personal evangelism. A soul under conviction has great difficulty in grasping the truth, or in yielding to it. His mind is

blinded and bound. A quiet attitude of victory over the opposing spirits has often brought swift release. A Filipino student was suspected of lying, but was resolutely standing by his falsehood. Quietly the position was taken: "In the name of the Lord, I rebuke these lying spirits." Suddenly the student broke down, confessed, and wept his way through to victory.[27]

You, too, can exercise authority over such hindering spirits, and trigger spiritual breakthroughs.

### You Have Authority to Bind and Loose

MacMillan recognized that Jesus gave to believers the authority to bind and loose demonic powers according to Matthew 16:19 and 18:18.[28] MacMillan records in his diary that they were "binding here and loosing there, but the work to be done is stupendous. Yet it can be done. Satan can be routed out of the strongholds where he is so deeply entrenched." He believed that if we "dwell in the secret place of the Most High," we can overcome the enemy. He further observed with perception in his journal, "Men, as God's mouthpieces, vary in value; not according to their ability, but according to the measure of their entire surrender. There are times, even today, when, like Elijah, we may say: 'There shall not . . . according to my word'—when our hearts, in full comprehension of God, bind and loose in definite power." This does not mean that we can bind and loose anything we desire. We must have assurance that it is the will of God and discernment that it is a demonic force with which we are dealing.[29]

MacMillan recognized that "while prayer precedes the exercise of authority, it does not take its place."[30] He describes this exercise of authority similar to Bounds' teaching on the "command of faith":

The command of faith is the divine means of moving mountains out of the way:

> "Ye shall say to this mountain, Be thou removed and be thou cast into the sea; and it shall obey you." The question involved is not that of an imposing faith, but that of an all-sufficient Name. . . . As he speaks to the mountain in the name of Christ, he puts his hand on the dynamic force that controls the universe. Heavenly energy is released, and his behest is obeyed.[31]

Practically speaking, then, we should not merely pray to God *about* our problems; we can speak an authoritative word in the name of Jesus *to* our problems.[32]

### Faith Accepts God's Will, Yet Wages War with the Enemy

Like Simpson and Murray, MacMillan believed that healing is a covenant privilege for the Christian. Therefore, we need to affirm it actively and strenuously: "We should claim this gracious relationship to the fullest degree for our own flesh and bones, and refuse the sicknesses that seek to fasten upon our physical frames."[33] He believed that illness and calamity are often the doing of the forces of Satan and are not to be accepted submissively as the will of God:

> It is ours to take hold jointly with the Spirit—for as He takes hold with us we must also cooperate with Him—against the things and the forces which assail our individual lives with a faithful and firm refusal of their right to control our bodies or our circumstances. Too often the Christian passively accepts whatever comes to him as being the will of the Lord, yielding without resistance at times to the wiles of the enemy himself. True faith in conflict is a steadfast and earnest will for

victory. . . . That "God hath spoken" is the ground upon which every forward step in the spiritual life must be taken.[34]

MacMillan knew this from experience. In early June 1928 Isabel became gravely ill. Her health plunged, and she was hospitalized and went through surgery. Several times Isabel came near to death, but after prayer she rallied.[35] At a time of crisis, MacMillan wrote in his distress, "Have prayed much for Divine interference, but, while grace to the spirit has been afforded, no definite release to the physical condition has been granted. In a sense I feel we have failed."

The following day, however, he rebuked himself, saying:

Yesterday, I wrote of failure—but that is not true. There is no failure to the soul that is united to God, and is living in the power of the age to come. Through all conflict, even through seeming defeat, we press on. God worketh and I work—but it is not I, but Christ Who liveth in me. What the Father is doing, I do. Therefore shall be accomplished all that He plans.[36]

This became a defining moment in MacMillan's spiritual growth and journey of faith. He came to terms with surrender to God through what some call "the prayer of relinquishment":

A few nights ago the question of submission to God's will was brought upon my spirit. After a period of careful examination, I was able to say that I am fully in acquiescence with the will of the Lord. I am not standing against Him. But He sent us here on His service; this service we are performing, and He is leading. I am confident that neither her work nor mine is done.[37]

Simultaneously, he realized that he was waging spiritual battle: "We are, by prayer in Jesus' name, dislodging the spirits that have bound the people of this field. It seems to me that an infernal fiat has gone forth that we must be crushed. But, 'rejoice not against me, O mine enemy; though I fall, I shall rise.' God is with us and we shall live and triumph."[38] He had an impression that forces of evil were trying to "wear out the saints of the Most High" (Daniel 7:25). MacMillan was ready to face Isabel's death, but he would struggle to the finish for her life.

How did MacMillan resolve the apparent contradiction of submission to God's will on one hand and aggressively fighting trials on the other? Later he reflected:

> As we come to know God better, everything takes on a different aspect to us, and we see God in all that comes. Not that we can accept each incident as from His hand. On the contrary, it may be directly from the enemy, and intended to harm us. But we can believe in His gracious providence, and know that, before it was permitted to come, it had to pass the inspection of His love and perfect wisdom. Thus we can give thanks for evil and for good alike, while at the same time positively resisting the devil, and refusing what comes to us from him.[39]

He did not believe it inconsistent to accept that God allows trials, yet simultaneously and forcefully engage the forces of evil that may be behind the trial.

### You Can Gain Victory Even in Seeming Failure and Loss

Ultimately, MacMillan's wife would be sacrificed for the sake of furthering the Gospel. One night when she was in a comatose state a massive earthquake shook the city. Because he was deeply concerned for the spiritual welfare of masses of Filipino people, MacMillan conducted an all-night prayer meeting. His resolve to shift the focal point of prayer from Isabel to unsaved souls keenly shows that his self-sacrificial love transcended the possibility of losing of his wife.

The next afternoon, their fourteenth wedding anniversary, Isabel died. How grief-stricken he must have been to lose the one he loved on the same date they started their life together. We can envision that the enemy assailed him with questions and doubts: "Where is your God now? What happened to this believer's authority you are supposed to be exercising?" Yet MacMillan wrote in his journal, "The event is one of the mysteries of our Christian experience, but we do not have to solve it. God doeth all things well." He came to realize that in God's eyes some people are ripe for the harvest and ready to go home to be with the Lord, having completed God's purposes for their lives. MacMillan understood that Isabel had arrived at that point. He also discerned that God was developing godly character in him.[40]

Isabel's passing was not a setback for MacMillan and the Filipino mission. Instead, it stirred the mission to greater unity and more intense prayer. His son Buchanan later remarked, "This seemed to be the beginning of a new era of spiritual life in the mission field, that has been singularly unresponsive and discouraging." MacMillan's loss resulted in the breaking of Satan's grip on the Filipinos. In little more than a year revival began to break out on the island, and eventually the mission became the largest and most successful evangelical Protestant ministry in the country. Jesus' words in John 12:24 became true of Isabel: Unless a grain of wheat falls into the ground and dies, it cannot bear fruit. Years later, MacMillan mused on the mysteries of unanswered prayer:

The enemy has been permitted occasion against him that his faith and spiritual preparedness may be proved upon the field of combat. The opportunity has come to "stand" (Eph. 6:13), and to triumph.

The answer which comes through some "terrible" thing, if we are abiding in God, is as truly from Him as that which men call a blessing. It may seem otherwise: our plans may be disrupted, our friends may be puzzled, our faith may be for the moment shaken. But its coming is a proof of His confidence in us, and an opportunity on our part to trust more fully and to glorify Him before the seen and the unseen world.[41]

While he did not understand, he had a sense of the sovereignty and timing of God—bringing closure to an era of his life and transition to a new era. MacMillan resumed his traveling ministry, evangelizing, exercising spiritual authority over demonic forces through power encounters and praying for the sick (many of whom were healed even though his wife was not). His faith did not waver; his vision did not fade; his authority did not diminish. And his ministry would grow greater in years to come.[42]

## We Must Not Misuse or Abuse the Believer's Authority

What would you do if someone did you wrong, like Cross did to MacMillan? MacMillan, though exercising authority, left in God's hands the manner in which *He* would carry out justice. He did not do as some today who claim the believer's authority, warning, "Touch not the Lord's anointed," and want to blow away their enemies with a curse. Rather, MacMillan cautioned not to misuse the believer's authority. He asserts that the authority of Jesus' name cannot be effective "in the mouth of an unspiritual disciple." Rather, only a "consecrated hand" can use the power of Christ's throne.[43] We must have no selfish motives, arrogant claims or acts or words of revenge.

In contrast to some contemporary faith teaching that has adapted his ideas, MacMillan did not teach that Jesus transferred *all* authority to believers: "In the world's long history, one Man only, with the unmeasured unction of the Holy Ghost upon Him, has been able to say, 'All authority hath been given unto me in heaven and in earth.'"[44] Rather, this delegated authority is not automatic, nor is it complete in this life, but will be fully in the Millennium, after Christ's coming. Nonetheless, MacMillan was also convinced that the Church has not yet attained the full capacity of its authority in this age.[45]

MacMillan stresses the importance of humility whenever we exercise authority and faith:

> So Jesus says, when you as servants have done all those things which are commanded you; when you have uprooted trees, removed mountains, healed the sick, led multitudes to salvation—remember that you are still servants of God. What you have done is simply what He has endued you with power to do, and what you have engaged to do for Him. You have not done aught of yourselves—all has been of His working.[46]

## You, Too, Can Exercise the Authority of the Believer!

You may be wondering, "Can I actually exercise the same authority as MacMillan? Is it really for every believer?" MacMillan would encourage you that it is *not* "the property only of a few elect souls. On the contrary, it is the possession of every true child of God. It is one of the 'all things' received in Christ."[47] If you are a believer in Jesus, no matter how weak or uneducated you think you are, you *are* able

205

through the cross of Christ and His victory to overcome sin, temptation, trial and the onslaughts of Satan.

## THINK AND DISCUSS

1. In what practical ways can you exercise the authority of the believer in your life?
2. Read John 1:12; Luke 10:19; Ephesians 1:19–23; 2:6. Discuss what it means to have the right to exercise spiritual authority.
3. Read Psalm 91. Under what conditions is it proper to claim divine protection?
4. Do you have family members who are not walking with God? Join together in prayer for them. How can you exercise the principles of authority in this chapter to claim their salvation?
5. Have you experienced excessive fear, depression, anger, addictions or hindrances to ministry? Do you think evil spirits may be harassing you? How can you overcome?
6. Read Matthew 12:28–29; 16:16–19; 18:18–20. Explain the authority of binding and loosing.
7. How do you know when to accept a trial as God's will and when to fight?
8. How can the believer's authority be misused?
9. Which of MacMillan's principles is the most helpful to you? Why?

## Read More about It

### Biographical

Paul L. King, *A Believer with Authority: The Life and Message of John A. MacMillan* (Camp Hill, Pa.: Christian Publications, 2001)

### Books by John MacMillan

*The Authority of the Believer* ( Harrisburg, Pa.: Christian Publications, 1980)

*Encounter with Darkness* (Harrisburg, Pa.: Christian Publications, 1980)

### Book about the Authority of the Believer

K. Neill Foster with Paul L. King, *Binding and Loosing: Exercising Authority over the Dark Powers* (Camp Hill, Pa.: Christian Publications, 1998)

# 12

## A. W. Tozer
### (1897–1963)

*Twentieth-Century Prophet and Mystic*

---

**Faith principle:**

*Faith pursues after God Himself.*

---

A. W. Tozer declared, "The only book that should ever be written is one that flows up from the heart, forced out by the inward pressure."[1] He believed, "You should never write a book unless you have to."[2] One day in 1948 Tozer found himself impelled to write. While waiting for a train at the LaSalle Street Station in Chicago to take him to a speaking engagement in McAllen, Texas, Tozer was immersed in thought. He was deeply burdened about the shallowness and superficiality of Christianity, and the need of believers to seek after God. Upon boarding the Pullman train, Tozer asked the porter for a small desk for his compartment. With no other resources except his Bible, he started to write:

In this hour of all-but-universal darkness, one cheering gleam appears: within the fold of conservative Christianity there are to be found increasing numbers of persons whose religious lives are marked by a growing hunger after God Himself. They are eager for spiritual realities and will not be put off with words, nor will they be content with correct "interpretations" of truth. They are athirst for God, and they will not be satisfied until they have drunk deep of the Fountain of Living Water.

This is the only real harbinger of revival which I have been able to detect anywhere on the religious horizon. It may be a cloud the size of a man's hand for which a few saints here and there have been looking. It can result in the resurrection of life for many souls and a recapture of that radiant wonder which should accompany faith in Christ, that wonder which has all but fled the Church of God in our day.[3]

As he knelt before the Lord the words flowed from his heart through his pen by the inspiration of the Holy Spirit. About 9:00 P.M. the porter came by with the last call for dinner. Tozer requested some tea and toast. "With only toast and tea to fortify him physically," his biographer described, "Tozer continued to write. He wrote all night long, the words coming to him as fast as he could jot them down. The manuscript was almost writing itself, so full of his subject was he."[4] When he arrived in McAllen early the next morning he had completed the rough draft of what would become his classic book *The Pursuit of God.* It described a life caught up in passion for God Himself, and nothing less.

## Meet A. W. Tozer

Converted at the age of seventeen by a lay preacher at a street meeting, Aiden Wilson Tozer attended the

Methodist Church and Church of the Brethren before he became ordained with The Christian and Missionary Alliance. He served as a pastor for 44 years in Stonewood and Morgantown, West Virginia, and in Indianapolis, Chicago and Toronto. A prolific writer, he became editor of *Alliance Life* for thirteen years. His writings and teachings have had an immense impact on the lives of thousands of Christians.

- His classic *The Pursuit of God* has sold more than 1.5 million copies and been translated into twenty languages. It was chosen by *Christianity Today* readers as one of the top ten most spiritually influential books.
- More than forty volumes of his writings and sermons have been published.
- Though he never went to high school (except for one day!), Tozer educated himself through insatiable reading of theological and classical Christian works and received two honorary doctorates.
- A man of deep prayer and worship, he frequently sought the Lord on his face for hours.
- Known as a twentieth-century prophet and "the conscience of evangelicalism," he proclaimed truths that both spoke to the times and transcend time.
- He has influenced many great Christian leaders, including Wilbur M. Smith, Warren Wiersbe and Leonard Ravenhill.
- He counseled great Christian leaders such as Billy Graham, Catherine Marshall and Senator Mark O. Hatfield.

When Tozer wrote an article or a book or a sermon, he wrote from the heart and the leading of the Holy Spirit. Through seeking the Lord in prayer he wrote and preached from receiving a "burden" from the Lord. Let us look at some of Tozer's principles for a faith that pursues after God.

## Have a Passion for Seeking After God

Tozer spoke of hungering and thirsting after God. This means having a passion for God and total devotion to Him. He sought to find people "who would join his Society of the Burning Heart."[5] He was always pressing onward and upward, deeper in God, praying, "O God, I have tasted of Thy goodness and it has both satisfied me and made me thirsty for more. . . . I want to want Thee; I long to be filled with longing; I thirst to be made more thirsty still. . . . Give me grace to rise and follow Thee up from this misty lowland where I have wandered so long."[6] His yearning after God is reflected in what he once told the great revival evangelist Leonard Ravenhill, "There are occasions when for hours I lay [sic] prostrate before God without saying a word of prayer or a word of praise—I just gaze on Him and worship."[7] While some people might consider that too emotional or undignified, it demonstrates Tozer's intensity and humility before God. Among Tozer's principles of worship are the following.

### WORSHIP IS THE MISSING JEWEL IN EVANGELICAL CHRISTIANITY

So wrote Tozer prophetically in the 1950s.[8] He felt that real worship was missing from the Church and needed to be restored. He would be pleased with the recent focus on adoration and praise of God, but he would be quite displeased with a lot of the fluff, self-centeredness and carnal spirituality that passes off as worship. Tozer defined worship the way he lived it: "Worship is to feel in your heart and to express in some appropriate manner a humbling but delightful sense of admiring awe and astonished wonder and overpowering love in the presence of that most ancient mystery, that majesty which philosophers call the First Cause but which we call our Father in heaven."[9]

### THE PRESENCE OF GOD IS MORE IMPORTANT THAN THE PROGRAM

So wrote Tozer in his book *The Root of the Righteous.*[10] More vital than following a routine or pattern or a programmed service, real worship is a personal encounter with the presence of God. Worship is not entertainment; it must be genuine. Our service for God must flow out of our fellowship with God: "Labor that does not spring out of worship is futile and can only be wood, hay and stubble in the day that shall try every man's work."[11]

It was said of Tozer, "He followed the cloud, not the calendar."[12] Tozer often got lost in the presence of God. On one occasion he was praying earnestly in his cabin at a camp conference where he was speaking and, lost in thought, did not notice the time. When it was his time to speak no one could find him, eventually asking someone else to speak in his place. After he finally showed up he remarked that he was occupied with another indispensable engagement.[13]

### GET CAUGHT UP IN THE AWESOMENESS OF GOD

When a young pastor, Tozer once went for a walk in the woods with another pastor to spend some time with the Lord in prayer and Bible reading. He related that the other man

stopped at a log, and if I know him, probably fell asleep. I went on a little farther, as Jesus did, and knelt down and began to read my Bible. I was reading about the camp of Israel in the wilderness and how God laid it out in a beautiful diamond pattern. All at once I saw God as I had never seen Him before. In that wooded sanctuary I fell on my face and worshiped. Since that experience, I have lost all interest in cheap religious thrills. The vacuous religious choruses we sing hold no attraction for me. I came face-to-face with the sovereign God, and since that time only God has mattered in my life.[14]

### SEEK GOD FOR HIMSELF, NOT FOR WHAT YOU CAN GET FROM HIM

There is a tendency among some today to exercise faith for themselves to become successful, prosperous or famous. Tozer warned that any motive for faith that is not centered in God and others, is for self. Worship is more important than fellowship: "You must be willing to give up your friends if you want to have the Friend."[15] He prayed:

O God, be Thou exalted over my possessions. Nothing of earth's treasures shall seem dear unto me if only Thou art glorified in my life. Be Thou exalted over my friendships. I am determined that Thou shalt be above all, though I must stand deserted and alone in the midst of the earth. Be Thou exalted above my comforts. Though it mean the loss of bodily comforts and the carrying of heavy crosses I shall keep my vow made this day before Thee. Be Thou exalted over my reputation. Make me ambitious to please Thee even if as a result I must sink into obscurity and my name be forgotten as a dream. Rise, O Lord, into Thy proper place of honor, above my ambitions, above my likes and dislikes, above my family, my health and even my life itself. Let me decrease that Thou mayest increase, let me sink that Thou mayest rise above.[16]

## You Can Be Confident of God's Will and Provision for Your Life

Like Müller, Tozer trusted God day by day to provide for his family, which grew to six boys and a girl. There were times in his early ministry, again like Müller, when he had to pray and trust God for food to eat that day. Then there would be a knock on the door, and a church member appeared with a bag of groceries.[17] He remarked of those times:

> Any of us who have experienced a life and ministry of faith can relate how the Lord has met our needs. My wife and I probably would have starved in those early years of ministry if we could not have trusted God completely for food and everything else. Of course, we are convinced that God can send money to His believing children—but it becomes a pretty cheap thing to get excited about the money and fail to give glory to Him who is the Giver![18]

He was never worried about what people thought or whether they might withhold finances if they were displeased with something he said or did:

> A few preachers have found a happy solution to the economic problem in the simple plan of living by faith. No one can put the economic squeeze on such a man; for he is accountable to God alone for his ministry. God is, by the same token, responsible for his daily bread. It is impossible to starve a man into submission under such an arrangement, for the servant of God lives on manna, and manna can be found wherever faith can see it.[19]

He believed there is no hardship in obeying God.

215

If we are in obedience to God we do not need to fear adverse circumstances or being out of God's will. Tozer encourages us:

> The man of true faith may live in the absolute assurance that his steps are ordered by the Lord. For him misfortune is out of the bounds of possibility. He cannot be torn from this earth one hour ahead of the time which God has appointed, and he cannot be detained on earth one moment after God is done with him here. He is not a waif of the wide world, a foundling of time and space, but a saint of the Lord and the darling of His particular care.[20]

## Seek Not Great Things for Yourself

Tozer learned from the early Church Father Ignatius, "Apart from Christ, let nothing dazzle you."[21] For His ordination, Tozer wrote an ordination covenant, to which he held throughout his life. In it he accepted humbly the prophetic mantle God had placed upon him, recognizing unpretentiously the honor of the anointing and his own unworthiness. He embodied the words of Jesus, "Whoever wishes to become great among you shall be your servant" (Matthew 20:26, NASB). It was both his prayer and his message:

> Anoint me with the oil of a New Testament prophet. Forbid that I should become a religious scribe and thus lose my prophetic calling. Save me from the curse that lies dark across the face of the modern clergy, the curse of compromise, of imitation, of professionalism. Save me from the error of judging a church by its size, its popularity or its amount of yearly offerings. Help me to remember that I am a prophet—not a promoter, not a religious manager, but a prophet. Let me never become a slave to crowds. Heal my soul of carnal ambitions and deliver me from the itch for publicity.[22]

Tozer's covenant with God was tested. There was a time after having built a new larger building in his rapidly growing church in Chicago that he began to take pride and satisfaction in what he had accomplished. He thought to himself, "The Pennsylvania farm boy had made it big in America's second largest city. The years of hard work were finally paying off." Immediately, he was convicted by the Holy Spirit of his pride and repented deeply of his attitude. He walked into every room of the new facility, surrendering each of them back to God.[23] No longer would he idolize big buildings and ministries. On another occasion he was introduced with great and lengthy accolades. When he came to the podium to speak he remarked with his wit, "Dear God, forgive him for what he said and forgive me for enjoying it so much."[24]

We would do well to adopt Tozer's prayer, "Lord, make me childlike. Deliver me from the urge to compete with another for prestige or position. I would be simple and artless as a little child. Deliver me from pose and pretense. Forgive me for thinking of myself. Help me to forget myself and find my true peace in beholding Thee."[25]

### In the Walk of Faith the Way Up Is Down

At the age of 42 after raising six boys, Tozer was blessed with a lovely daughter. He adored her but, although he had dedicated her to the Lord, came to realize he regarded her as his own. He related that this became a pivotal point in his walk with God:

> The day came when I had to die to my Becky, my little Rebecca. I had to give her up and turn her over to God to take if He wanted her at any time. She has been His ever since. When I made that awful, terrible dedication

I didn't know but that God would take her from me. But he didn't. . . . She was safer after I gave her up than she ever had been before. If I had clung to her I would have jeopardized her; but when I opened my hands and said with tears, "You can have her, God, the dearest thing I have," she became perfectly safe.[26]

Out of his own experience Tozer came to believe that the walk of faith involves dying to ourselves so that God can use us. He emphasized the "Crucified Life." He prayed, "Show us how to die that we might rise again to newness of life. Rend the veil of our self life from the top down as Thou didst rend the veil of the temple. We would draw near in full assurance of faith."[27] He believed that only people who have been broken and have died to themselves can truly be used greatly by God.

As a young pastor Tozer had high ambitions for his church and grand desires of what he could accomplish for God. Tozer's church in Indianapolis was growing, yet for a wealthy and influential church member it was not growing fast enough or big enough. So the parishioner left and started another church down the street. It was a dark and difficult time for Tozer. He poured out his heart in tears to the Lord, feeling inadequate and asking why this was happening to him. God led him to Exodus 23 where He promised the Israelites they would overcome their adversaries and enter the Promised Land: "But I will not drive them out in a single year. . . . Little by little I will drive them out before you, until you have increased enough to take possession of the land" (verses 29–30, NIV). God was assuring him these dark days would not last. He sensed the Lord telling him, "Son, if I give you a big wide ministry right away, you will blow up. So I will take you a little at a time, and I will enlarge you a little at a time."[28]

Out of that painful episode he penned "Five Vows of Spiritual Power." These vows are vital to our faith:

1. *Deal thoroughly with sin.* . . . This is to say that every known sin is to be named, identified and repudiated, and that we must trust God for deliverance from it, so that there is no conscious, deliberate sin anywhere in our lives. It is absolutely necessary that we deal thus, because God is a holy God and sin is on the throne of the world. So don't call your sins by some other name. If you're jealous, call it jealousy. If you tend to pity yourself and feel that you are not appreciated, but are like a flower born to blush unseen and waste your sweetness on the desert air, call it what it is—self-pity. . . .

2. *Never own anything.* I do not mean by this that you cannot have things. I mean that you ought to get delivered from the sense of possessing them. This sense of possessing is what hinders us. All babies are born with their fists clenched, and it seems to me it means: "This is mine!" One of the first things they say is "mine" in an angry voice. That sense of "This is mine" is a very injurious thing to the spirit. If you can get rid of it so that you have no feeling of possessing anything, there will come a great sense of freedom and liberty into your life. . . .

3. *Never defend yourself.* We are all born with a desire to defend ourselves. And if you insist upon defending yourself, God will let you do it. But if you turn the defense of yourself over to God He will defend you. . . .

4. *Never pass anything on about anybody else that will hurt him.* . . . If you know something that would hinder or hurt the reputation of one of

God's children, bury it forever. Find a little garden out back, a little spot somewhere—and when
somebody comes around with an evil story, take
it out and bury it. . . . If you want God to be good
to you, you are going to have to be good to His
children. . . .

5. *Never accept any glory.* God is jealous of His glory
and He will not give His glory to another. He will not
even share His glory with another. . . . That is very
dangerous ground—seeking a reputation among
the saints. It's bad enough to seek a reputation in
the world, but it's worse to seek a reputation among
the people of God. Our Lord gave up His reputation, and so must we.[29]

## Truth Has Two Wings

Tozer recognized that in the life of faith, as in all of
the Christian life, there needs to be a balance of truth.
He expressed it in the motto "Truth has two wings":
"Truth is like a bird; it cannot fly on one wing. Yet we
are forever trying to take off with one wing flapping
furiously and the other tucked neatly out of sight. . . .
Let's use both wings. We'll get further that way."[30] He
cautioned, "Overstress the minors and you have chaos;
overlook the majors and you have death."[31] Because
of lack of balance, he emphasized the need to restore
neglected truths, especially missions, prophecy, divine
healing, holiness, the Holy Spirit, victory over self and
sin, and worship.[32]

Hence, regarding many debated doctrines in Scripture he maintained they are both-and, not either-or.
He was therefore not a Calvinist, nor an Arminian,
but a "Cal-minian." When asked what he believed
about predestination and free will he replied he was
an Arminian when he preached and a Calvinist when

he prayed. He believed in both order and structure in church worship and also freedom for the Spirit of God to move, in both emotion and decorum. Between the two extremes regarding spiritual gifts, he was neither dispensational (believing the gifts are not continuing in the Church today) nor Pentecostal (believing tongues is the initial evidence of the fullness of the Spirit). He believed missing supernatural gifts of the Spirit was a "tragedy in the church."[33] Regarding the end times, he did not get embroiled in debates as to whether the rapture will take place before, after or in the middle of the tribulation. Although he did not accept much of Roman Catholic theology, he nonetheless enjoyed and immersed himself in the writings of Roman Catholic saints and mystics who walked close to God. He even corresponded with Thomas Merton, a Trappist monk who shared Tozer's love for the mystical life.

Tozer counseled a young ministerial student not to get caught up in debates or major on the minors. Instead, he advised, "Go to your room and meet God. At the end of four years you will be way down the line and they'll still be where they started, because greater minds than yours have wrestled with this problem and have not come up with satisfactory conclusions. Instead, learn to know God."[34]

## Faith Must Be Sound—Not All Faith Pleases God

During his many years as a pastor Tozer encountered numerous strange things said and done in the name of faith. He acknowledged that "without faith it is impossible to please God" (Hebrews 11:6, NIV), but he also commented, "Not all faith pleases God."[35] He counsels that faith must be sound to be strong. His keys to a strong, sound faith include the following:

- *Beware of having faith in your own faith:* "Faith in faith is faith astray."[36]
- *Faith must rest on the character of God, not His promises:* "Faith must rest in confidence upon the one who makes the promises."[37]
- *Faith looks to God, not to anything or anyone else*: "Faith is . . . a continuous gaze of the heart at the Triune God. . . . Faith is a redirecting of our sight, a getting out of the focus of our own vision and getting God into focus."[38]
- *Faith and reason are not opposed, but faith is beyond reason:* "Faith never goes contrary to reason; faith simply ignores reason and rises above it."[39]
- *Faith must be based on right thinking:* "To be right, we must think right. What we think about when we are free to think about what we will—that is what we are or will soon become."[40]
- *True faith involves obedience:* Tozer was not concerned about getting emotional responses but rather getting people to act their faith through obedience to God. Once while preaching in Long Beach, California, Tozer stirred the congregation. People were expecting a large altar call, but at the close of his message, he instructed the congregation, "Don't come down here to the altar and cry about it—go home and live it."[41]
- *Study and emulate the faith of great Christian devotional writers of the past:* Tozer called such people his friends and friends of God—people like Brother Lawrence, François Fénelon, Madame Guyon, Bernard of Clairvaux, Thomas à Kempis, among many others. He remarked, "These people know God and I want to know what they know about God and how they came to know it."[42]

## You, Too, Can Have a Heart That Seeks After God!

A. W. Tozer's faith came from seeking God with all his heart above all else and putting nothing ahead of God. You can do the same. Tozer invites you to pray with him: "O Lord, I have heard a good word inviting me to look away to Thee and be satisfied. My heart longs to respond, but sin has clouded my vision till I see Thee but dimly. Be pleased to cleanse me in Thine own precious blood, and make me inwardly pure, so that I may with unveiled eyes gaze upon Thee all the days of my earthly pilgrimage."[43]

## Think and Discuss

1. In what practical ways can you seek after God?
2. How can you have confidence in God's will and leading in your life?
3. Do you find yourself seeking recognition? How can you seek great things for God, on one hand, and be willing to abandon your ambitions, on the other hand?
4. In what ways can you see God taking you up through the down experiences in your life? How is God enlarging you little by little?
5. What are some of the beliefs and practices of the Christian faith that often lack balance? How can that balance be restored?
6. Discuss some of the ways a person's faith may be unsound.
7. Which of Tozer's principles is the most helpful to you? Why?

## READ MORE A BOUT IT

### Biographical

David J. Fant, *A. W. Tozer: A Twentieth-Century Prophet* (Harrisburg, Pa.: Christian Publications, 1964)

James L. Snyder, *In Pursuit of God: The Life of A. W. Tozer* (Camp Hill, Pa.: Christian Publications, 1991)

### Books by A. W. Tozer

Warren W. Wiersbe, compiler, *The Best of A. W. Tozer* (Camp Hill, Pa.: Christian Publications, 1978, 1980), vols. 1, 2

*Faith beyond Reason* (Camp Hill, Pa.: Christian Publications, 1989)

*Jesus, Author of Our Faith* (Camp Hill, Pa.: Christian Publications, 1988)

*The Pursuit of God* (Harrisburg, Pa.: Christian Publications, 1948)

*Worship: The Missing Jewel* (Camp Hill, Pa.: Christian Publications, 1992)

### Devotional Books by A. W. Tozer

Gerald B. Smith, compiler, *Renewed Day by Day* (Camp Hill, Pa.: Christian Publications, 1980, 1991), vols. 1, 2

Edythe Draper, compiler, *The Pursuit of God: A 31 Day Experience* (Camp Hill, Pa.: Christian Publications, 1995)

# Epilogue

Regardless of your church background and beliefs, you can learn from these great evangelical leaders how to walk in faith. These men and women of faith come from many denominational backgrounds: Anglican, Baptist, Brethren, Christian and Missionary Alliance, Dutch Reformed, Methodist, Presbyterian, Quaker. They would not all agree on all matters of doctrine and theology. But they do show us how to exercise a healthy faith that is both strong and sound.

From George Müller you can learn to depend on God fully. You can join with Hudson Taylor in the supernatural adventure of faith. Through insights from Charles Spurgeon you can grow a faith that overcomes the challenges in your life. From Phoebe Palmer you can learn to trust the Lord with a full surrender to Him. Like Hannah Whitall Smith you can learn the secret of a happy life in the midst of trials and tragedies. E. M. Bounds teaches you how to unleash the powerful force of believing prayer. Andrew Murray encourages you to claim your inheritance in Christ. A. B. Simpson shows you valuable keys to wholeness of life. Oswald Chambers gives you nuggets of wisdom for a faith of uncommon sense. Amy Carmichael shows you that you really can hear from God. John MacMillan exhorts you to exercise your authority as a believer. A. W. Tozer leads you into pursuing after God Himself above all else.

These are only a few of the men and women of mighty faith. We can learn from the lives of many others:

- Dwight Moody, the popular nineteenth-century evangelist and founder of Moody Bible Institute, and his associate R. A. Torrey
- friends of Charles Spurgeon: Baptist Holiness leader F. B. Meyer and Spurgeon's interim successor A. T. Pierson, Presbyterian Holiness leader
- Presbyterian T. J. McCrossan, a former Greek professor
- pastor/evangelist F. F. Bosworth
- Presbyterian Higher Life leader William Boardman
- Episcopalian medical doctor and healing evangelist Charles Cullis
- Welsh revival leaders Evan Roberts and Jessie Penn-Lewis
- Methodist Holiness preacher George D. Watson
- Presbyterian evangelist Charles Finney
- popular Baptist pastor A. J. Gordon, founder of Gordon College and what later became Gordon-Conwell Seminary
- popular Bible teacher and YMCA leader S. D. Gordon
- Thomas Upham, philosopher and early psychologist of faith
- Chinese spiritual leader Watchman Nee
- Mrs. Charles Cowman, missionary to Japan and popular devotional writer

- Dorothea Trudel, early Swiss healing pioneer
- Johann Christoph Blumhardt, Lutheran leader with healing and spiritual warfare ministries
- Paul Rader, evangelist and author of the songs "Only Believe" and "Old Time Power"
- famous cricket player turned missionary C. T. Studd
- healing leader and hymnwriter (author of "Standing on the Promises") R. K. Carter
- evangelist Charles Price
- Carrie Judd Montgomery, journalist of faith and bridge-builder between Pentecostals and non-Pentecostals

And the list could go on. Some of these names may be familiar to you; others are relatively unknown. But all these taught and practiced many of the same principles and other similar concepts of faith. By reading these classic leaders of faith and emulating their principles and faith walk, you, too, can live with great faith that is both strong and sound!

# Notes

## Chapter 1

1. George Müller, *The Autobiography of George Müller* (New Kensington, Pa.: Whitaker Books, 1984), 227–229. Quotes from this book are used by permission of the publisher.

2. Arthur T. Pierson, a respected scholar and interim successor to the pulpit of Charles Spurgeon, was so impressed with Müller's faith and ministry that he wrote the first full biography of Müller. Pierson claimed that almost every form of "faith work" can be traced to Müller or the example of his spiritual predecessor A. H. Francke. He observed, "The passion of George Müller's soul was to know fully the secrets of prevailing with God and man." A. T. Pierson, *George Müller of Bristol* (New York: Fleming H. Revell, 1899), 138, 354.

3. Ibid., 228–229.

4. Ibid., 229.

5. Ibid., 229–230.

6. George Müller, *Autobiography of George Müller: The Life of Trust*, ed. H. Lincoln Wayland (Grand Rapids: Baker Book House, 1981), 235.

7. Müller, *Autobiography*, 212. Used by permission of the publisher, Whitaker House.

8. Pierson, *George Müller of Bristol*, 82.

9. Müller, *Autobiography*, 42. Used by permission of the publisher, Whitaker House.

10. Ibid., 226.

11. Pierson, *George Müller of Bristol*, 81.

12. Müller, *Autobiography*, 206.

13. Pierson, *George Müller of Bristol*, 23.

14. Ibid., 141, 272.

15. Quoted in Mrs. Charles Cowman, *Streams in the Desert* (Grand Rapids: Zondervan, 1925, 1972), vol. 1, 165.

16. Ibid., 117.

17. Müller, *Autobiography*, 43. Used by permission of the publisher, Whitaker House.

18. Ibid., 182.

19. Ibid., 68.

20. Pierson, *George Müller of Bristol*, 55–56, 141.

21. *The Christian and Missionary Alliance Weekly*, 9 February 1907, 64.

22. Müller, *Autobiography*, 171–172, 175. Used by permission of the publisher, Whitaker House.

23. Ibid., 175.

24. Pierson, *George Müller of Bristol*, 127.

25. Müller, *Autobiography*, 44. Used by permission of the publisher, Whitaker House.

26. R. A. Torrey, *The Power of Prayer* (Grand Rapids: Zondervan, 1971), 124–125.

27. Roger Steer, *George Müller: Delighted in God!* (Wheaton: Harold Shaw Publishers, 1975), 265–266.

28. Ibid., 266–267.

29. Roger Steer, *Spiritual Secrets of George Müller* (Wheaton: Harold Shaw Publishers, 1985), 104–105.

30. Müller, *Autobiography*, 43, 162. Used by permission of the publisher, Whitaker House.

31. Steer, *Spiritual Secrets*, 87.

32. Müller, *Autobiography*, 195–196. Used by permission of the publisher, Whitaker House.

33. Steer, *Spiritual Secrets*, 88.

34. Müller, *Autobiography*, 154–157. Used by permission of the publisher, Whitaker House.

## Chapter 2

1. Howard and Geraldine Taylor, *Hudson Taylor in Early Years* (London: China Inland Mission, 1911, 1930), 164–169.

2. Pierson, *George Müller of Bristol*, 354.

3. Cited in Andrew Murray, *Key to the Missionary Problem*, contemporized by Leona Choy (Fort Washington, Pa.: Christian Literature Crusade, 1979), 88.

4. Leslie T. Lyall, *A Passion for the Impossible: The China Inland Mission 1865–1965* (Chicago: Moody Press, 1965), 43.

5. Howard and Geraldine Taylor, *Hudson Taylor's Spiritual Secret* (Chicago: Moody Press, 1932), 117–118; Howard Taylor, *Early Years*, 478–479, 488.

6. Taylor and Taylor, *Spiritual Secret*, 19.

7. J. Hudson Taylor, *Union and Communion with Christ* (Minneapolis: Bethany House Publishers, n.d.), 20.

8. Taylor and Taylor, *Spiritual Secret,* 19–20.

9. Ibid., 229.

10. Ibid., 156.

11. Taylor, *Union and Communion,* 46.

12. Taylor and Taylor, *Spiritual Secret,* 32; *Early Years,* 131, 132, 137.

13. Taylor and Taylor, *Early Years,* 131.

14. Ibid., 131–135.

15. Taylor and Taylor, *Spiritual Secret,* 38, 120; *Early Years,* 491; Bill Gothard, *Men's Manual* (Oak Brook, Ill.: Institute in Basic Youth Conflicts, 1983), vol. 2, 84; Lyall, *Passion for the Impossible,* 38.

16. Taylor and Taylor, *Early Years,* 188.

17. Ibid., 188–191.

18. Ibid., 196–198.

19. Ibid., 191.

20. Lyall, *Passion for the Impossible,* 43; V. Raymond Edman, *They Found the Secret* (Grand Rapids: Zondervan, 1960), 19.

21. J. Hudson Taylor, "Reckon on God's Faithfulness," *Triumphs of Faith,* July 1902, 159.

22. F. F. Bosworth, *Christ the Healer* (Grand Rapids: Fleming H. Revell, 1948, 1973), 185; *Oswald Chambers: His Life and Work* (London: Simpkin Marshall, 1941), 53; F. B. Meyer, *Five Musts of the Christian Life* (Chicago: Moody Press, 1927), 91ff.; *The Secret of Guidance* (Chicago: Moody Press, n.d.), 50. Many other evangelical leaders also taught trusting in God's faith, including Charles Spurgeon, A. B. Simpson and Andrew Murray.

23. Taylor, *Union and Communion,* 9–10.

24. Taylor and Taylor, *Spiritual Secret,* 236.

25. J. Hudson Taylor, quoted in Pierson, *George Müller of Bristol,* 145.

26. Roger Steer, "Pushing Inward," *Christian History* 52 (Vol. XV, No. 4), 10.

27. Taylor and Taylor, *Spiritual Secret,* 30.

28. Lyall, *Passion for the Impossible,* 34.

29. Hudson Taylor, *Union and Communion,* 42.

30. Marshall Broomhall, *By Love Compelled: The Call of the China Inland Mission* (London: Hodder & Stoughton, 1936), 14.

31. Lyall, *Passion for the Impossible,* 8.

32. Murray, *Key to the Missionary Problem,* 87, 103, 107.

33. Lyall, *Passion for the Impossible,* 11.

## Chapter 3

1. Lewis Drummond, *Spurgeon: Prince of Preachers* (Grand Rapids: Kregel, 1992), 221. Spurgeon also makes reference to this in *Faith's Checkbook* (Chicago: Moody Press, n.d.), 50.

2. Drummond, *Spurgeon,* 420.

3. Charles H. Spurgeon, *What the Holy Spirit Does in a Believer's Life,* comp. and ed. Robert Hall (Lynnwood, Wash.: Emerald Books, 1993), 14,

51–52. Spurgeon's interim successor, Dr. A. T. Pierson, also affirmed the reality and importance of supernatural power: "A supernatural gospel is meant to accomplish supernatural results, and needs a supernatural power behind it and its messengers." A. T. Pierson, *The Acts of the Holy Spirit* (Harrisburg, Pa.: Christian Publications, 1980), 92. At the same time, "Spurgeon, not given to unscriptural mystical experiences, placed little worth on supernatural accounts that had no basis in the Bible." Drummond, *Spurgeon*, 235.

Living before the advent of Pentecostalism, he leaned toward believing that the gift of tongues was temporary but did not rule out the possibility as long as the emphasis was not on the gift: "Even if you could obtain miraculous gifts, you ought not to be satisfied to speak with tongues or to work miracles, but you should press on to know the Spirit within—indwelling, communing, quickening you." Spurgeon, *What the Holy Spirit Does*, 128; see also 97, 104.

4. Drummond, *Spurgeon*, 181, 184, 235–236, 281.

5. Ibid., 81.

6. Russell H. Conwell, *Life of Charles Haddon Spurgeon: The World's Great Preacher* (Philadelphia: Edgewood Publishing, 1892), 181–182.

7. Drummond, *Spurgeon*, 167.

8. Ibid., 91.

9. Ibid., 173.

10. Ibid., 271; see also 284.

11. Conwell, *Life of Charles Haddon Spurgeon*, 173.

12. Ibid., 186.

13. Charles H. Spurgeon, *Triumph of Faith in a Believer's Life*, comp. and ed. Robert Hall (Lynnwood, Wash.: Emerald Books, 1994), 68.

14. Charles H. Spurgeon, *Morning by Morning* (Old Tappan, N.J.: Fleming H. Revell, 1984), 294.

15. Ibid., 100.

16. Spurgeon, *Faith's Checkbook*, 139.

17. Charles H. Spurgeon, *The Power of Prayer in a Believer's Life*, comp. and ed. Robert Hall (Lynnwood, Wash.: Emerald Books, 1993), 43; Charles H. Spurgeon, *1000 Devotional Thoughts* (Grand Rapids: Baker Book House, 1976), 443.

18. Spurgeon, *Morning by Morning*, 240.

19. Charles H. Spurgeon, *Metropolitan Tabernacle Pulpit* (Pasadena, Tex.: Pilgrim Publications, 1979), vol. 7, 548.

20. Spurgeon, *Metropolitan Tabernacle Pulpit*, vol. 36, 478.

21. Charles H. Spurgeon, *All of Grace* (Springdale, Pa.: Whitaker House, 1981, 1983), 45.

22. Charles H. Spurgeon, *Spiritual Warfare in a Believer's Life*, comp. and ed. Robert Hall (Lynnwood, Wash.: Emerald Books, 1993), 156.

23. Spurgeon, *What the Holy Spirit Does*, 36; *Triumph of Faith in a Believer's Life*, 35.

24. Drummond, *Spurgeon*, 749.

25. Conwell, *Life of Charles Haddon Spurgeon*, 182, 354, 357–359, 361.

26. Spurgeon, *Spiritual Warfare in a Believer's Life*, 168.
27. Spurgeon, *Power of Prayer in a Believer's Life*, 114.
28. Spurgeon, *1000 Devotional Thoughts*, 36; *Morning by Morning*, 253.
29. Spurgeon, *Power of Prayer in a Believer's Life*, 69.
30. Spurgeon, *Faith's Checkbook*, 44.
31. Conwell, *Life of Charles Haddon Spurgeon*, 349–350.
32. Spurgeon, *Morning by Morning*, 312.
33. Spurgeon, *Triumph of Faith*, 100.
34. Charles H. Spurgeon, *1000 Devotional Thoughts*, 341. Spurgeon's devotional book *Faith's Checkbook* is based on this premise that the promises of God are appropriated by faith—as in endorsing and cashing a check.
35. Spurgeon, quoted in Mrs. Charles Cowman, *Streams in the Desert* (Grand Rapids: Zondervan, 1925, 1972), vol. 1, 64.
36. Spurgeon, *Morning by Morning*, 80.
37. Spurgeon, *Triumph of Faith*, 63.
38. Spurgeon, *Morning by Morning*, 319.
39. Spurgeon, quoted in *Streams in the Desert*, 114.
40. Drummond, *Spurgeon*, 464.
41. Ibid., 462.
42. Ibid., 559.
43. Spurgeon, *1000 Devotional Thoughts*, 470.
44. Spurgeon, *Faith's Checkbook*, 28; *Morning by Morning*, 335.
45. Spurgeon, *All of Grace*, 86.
46. Spurgeon, *Spiritual Warfare in a Believer's Life*, 176.
47. Ibid., 157–159.
48. Spurgeon, quoted in Mrs. Charles Cowman, *Streams in the Desert* (Grand Rapids: Zondervan, 1966), vol. 2, 13 January.
49. Spurgeon, *Triumph of Faith*, 60; see also 34.
50. Spurgeon, *Faith's Checkbook*, 5.
51. Conwell, *Life of Charles Haddon Spurgeon*, 255, 258.
52. Spurgeon, *Morning by Morning*, 26 October.
53. Ibid., 5.
54. Spurgeon, *Triumph of Faith*, 87.
55. Spurgeon, *All of Grace*, 55–56.
56. Spurgeon, *Triumph of Faith*, 26.
57. Spurgeon, *Morning by Morning*, 80, 295.

## Chapter 4

1. Charles Edward White, *The Beauty of Holiness* (Grand Rapids: Francis Asbury Press, 1986), 5–9.
2. Harold E. Raser, *Phoebe Palmer: Her Life and Thought* (Lewiston, N.Y.: Edwin Mellen Press, 1987), 1.
3. Ibid., 118.
4. Among these leaders, B. T. Roberts received a second blessing of sanctification through her ministry, which became a foundational stone for

his founding of the Free Methodist Church. Thomas Upham (1799–1872), a Congregational professor of mental and moral philosophy at Bowdoin College, Brunswick, Maine, became a Methodist Holiness leader after contact with Phoebe Palmer. At one of her meetings he experienced the sanctifying baptism in the Spirit, which he described as "the beginning of days," like a second conversion. Raser, *Phoebe Palmer,* 53. Upham became the nineteenth-century "Philosopher of Faith" with his 300-plus-page book *The Life of Faith* (Boston, Mass.: Waite, Pierce, 1845; New York: Garland Press, 1984). Along with Palmer's *Faith and its Effects* (New York: Palmer and Hughes, 1848, 1869), these two books were the most comprehensive on the subject of faith in the mid-nineteenth century and influenced much of nineteenth and early twentieth-century thinking on faith, including C&MA leaders A. B. Simpson and A. W. Tozer. A. B. Simpson adapted Palmer's teaching on positive confession, modifying Palmer's terminology "professing the blessing" to "confessing the blessing." Episcopalian medical doctor Charles Cullis (d. 1892) also received the sanctifying baptism in the Spirit through the ministry of Phoebe Palmer in 1862. After reading a book about the life of Dorothea Trudel in 1869, he began a ministry of faith and healing, based on Palmer's teaching that "the promise does not hinge on feeling, but believing." Hannah Whitall Smith in her book *The Christian's Secret of a Happy Life* (Old Tappan, N.J.: Fleming H. Revell, 1942) shows evidences of influence by Phoebe Palmer. In addition, according to two scholars of the holiness and Pentecostal movements, Donald Dayton and Vinson Synan, Palmer's teachings and practices served as a forerunner of the Pentecostal movement. See Donald W. Dayton, *Theological Roots of the Pentecostal Movement* (Peabody, Mass.: Hendrickson Publishers, 1987); and Vinson Synan, *The Holiness-Pentecostal Tradition* (Grand Rapids: Wm. B. Eerdmans, 1997), 17–19, 27, 32.

5. Raser, *Phoebe Palmer,* 48.

6. Ibid., 151.

7. Dayton, *Theological Roots,* 94.

8. White, *Beauty of Holiness,* 47.

9. Raser, *Phoebe Palmer,* 185.

10. Ibid.

11. Ibid., 112.

12. White, *Beauty of Holiness,* 167.

13. Ibid., 21.

14. Peter C. Erb, *Pietists: Selected Writings* (New York: Paulist Press, 1983), 239–241.

15. Palmer, *Faith and its Effects,* 113, 296, 327. Years later, A. B. Simpson adapted and echoed Palmer's teaching: "Faith is not only believing, but confessing its confidence. . . . So we must not only claim, but confess our blessings, and regard the things which are still future as accomplished in God's purpose." A. B. Simpson, *Christ in the Bible* (Camp Hill, Pa.: Christian Publications, 1992), vol. 1, 80. (See chapter 8 in this book, on A. B. Simpson, for more information.) So the popular phrase "confessing your blessing" is not original with modern faith teachers but with Palmer and

Simpson (and other classic leaders such as Charles Spurgeon and Hannah Whitall Smith as well).

16. Palmer, *Faith and its Effects*, 327.
17. Ibid., 31.
18. Ibid., 189–190.
19. Raser, *Phoebe Palmer*, 185.
20. Ibid., 60, 62.
21. White, *Beauty of Holiness*, 69.
22. Raser, *Phoebe Palmer*, 181.
23. White, *Beauty of Holiness*, 9.
24. Ibid., 22.
25. Ibid., 21–23.
26. Ibid., 172.
27. Raser, *Phoebe Palmer*, 57.
28. White, *Beauty of Holiness*, 175.
29. Ibid., 174.
30. Ibid.
31. Ibid., 12, 17.

## Chapter 5

1. Marie Henry, *Hannah Whitall Smith* (Minneapolis: Bethany House Publishers, 1984), 79–83. Excerpts from this book used by permission of Bethany House Publishers, a division of Baker Book House.
2. Ibid., 83.
3. Ibid., 84–86.
4. Ibid., 87.
5. Hannah Whitall Smith, *Everyday Religion* (Chicago: Moody Press, 1966), 90.
6. Hannah Whitall Smith, *The Unselfishness of God* (Princeton: Littlebrook Publishing, 1987), 189. See also Hannah Whitall Smith, *Living Confidently in God's Love* (New Kensington, Pa.: Whitaker House, 1984), 261.
7. Hannah Whitall Smith, *The Christian's Secret of a Happy Life* (Old Tappan, N.J.: Fleming H. Revell, 1942), 15.
8. Smith, *Living Confidently*, 172–173.
9. Ibid., 175–176, 262.
10. Smith, *Unselfishness of God*, 191–196.
11. Smith, *Christian's Secret*, 52.
12. Ibid., 32.
13. Smith, *Unselfishness of God*, 15–16.
14. Smith, *Christian's Secret*, 36.
15. Hannah Whitall Smith, *God of All Comfort* (Chicago: Moody Press, 1956), 246, 249, 252–253.
16. Smith, *Unselfishness of God*, 187.
17. Henry, *Hannah Whitall Smith*, 87.
18. Smith, *Christian's Secret*, 83.

19. Ibid., 101.
20. Henry, *Hannah Whitall Smith*, 87.
21. Smith, *Living Confidently*, 206–207.
22. Henry, *Hannah Whitall Smith*, 129.
23. Smith, *Living Confidently*, 97.
24. Smith, *Christian's Secret*, 53.
25. Smith, *Living Confidently*, 132.
26. Ibid., 63.
27. Smith, *Christian's Secret*, 81–83.
28. Smith, *Living Confidently*, 113.
29. Ibid., 142, 146.
30. Smith, *Christian's Secret*, 83.
31. Smith, *Living Confidently*, 261.
32. Ibid., 261.
33. Smith, *Unselfishness of God*, 190; *Living Confidently*, 260–261.
34. Smith, *Christian's Secret*, 67.
35. Ibid., 69.
36. Ibid., 59.
37. Henry, *Hannah Whitall Smith*, 82; some believed this was the evidence of the baptism or filling of the Holy Spirit.
38. Ibid., 130.
39. Ibid., 157.
40. Ibid.
41. Ibid., 89.

## Chapter 6

1. Lyle Wesley Dorsett, *E. M. Bounds: Man of Prayer* (Grand Rapids: Zondervan, 1991), 17–18. Used by permission of Lyle Wesley Dorsett.
2. Ibid., 19.
3. Ibid. It is noteworthy that even though Bounds ended up serving the South in the Civil War, in his later writings he exalts the prayer life and holiness of William Wilberforce, the British statesman who campaigned in England against slavery. See E. M. Bounds, *Purpose in Prayer* (Chicago: Moody Press, n.d.), 70–73.
4. Dorsett, *E. M. Bounds*, 26. Used by permission of Lyle Wesley Dorsett.
5. Bounds, *Purpose in Prayer*, 31–32.
6. Ibid., 38.
7. Ibid., 77, 82, 86–88, 94.
8. Ibid., 80, 86, 96.
9. Dorsett, *E. M. Bounds*, 51. Used by permission of Lyle Wesley Dorsett.
10. Bounds, *Purpose in Prayer*, 41.
11. Ibid., 91.
12. Ibid., 94.

13. E. M. Bounds, *Power through Prayer* (Grand Rapids: Baker Book House, 1978), 64.

14. Ibid., 102, 106.

15. Ibid., 124.

16. Ibid., 118–119.

17. Dorsett, *E. M. Bounds*, 57. Used by permission of Lyle Wesley Dorsett.

18. Bounds, *Purpose in Prayer*, 9, 78, 80.

19. Bounds, *Power through Prayer*, 111.

20. Dorsett, *E. M. Bounds*, 28. Used by permission of Lyle Wesley Dorsett.

21. Bounds, *Purpose in Prayer*, 24. Again he says, "To a prayerful man God is present in realized force." Ibid., 9.

22. Bounds, *Power through Prayer*, 64.

23. Ibid., 98–99.

24. Ibid., 99.

25. Ibid., 100.

26. E. M. Bounds, *Book 1: The Necessity of Prayer*, from *The Complete Works of E. M. Bounds* (Grand Rapids: Baker Book House, 1990), 43.

27. Ibid., 39.

28. Ibid., 43.

29. Brad Young, *Jesus the Jewish Theologian* (Peabody, Mass.: Hendrickson Publishers, 1995), 172.

30. Dorsett, *E. M. Bounds*, 38. Used by permission of Lyle Wesley Dorsett.

31. Bounds, *Necessity of Prayer*, 45.

32. Ibid., 38.

33. Dorsett, *E. M. Bounds*, 51. Used by permission of Lyle Wesley Dorsett.

34. Ibid., 46.

35. Ibid., 60.

36. E. M. Bounds, *Winning the Invisible War* (Springdale, Pa.: Whitaker House, 1984), 151.

37. Bounds, *Purpose in Prayer*, 24.

38. Ibid., 24.

39. Ibid., 45.

40. Bounds, *Winning the Invisible War*, 151.

41. Ibid., 152.

42. Charles H. Spurgeon, *The Power of Prayer in a Believer's Life*, comp. and ed. Robert Hall (Lynnwood, Wash.: Emerald Books, 1993), 67.

43. A. T. Pierson, *Lessons in the School of Prayer* (Dixon, Mo.: Rare Christian Books, n.d.), 60–61. (See also Chapter 11 in this book, on John MacMillan.)

44. E. M. Bounds, *Prayer and Praying Men* (Grand Rapids: Baker Book House, 1977), 148.

45. Bounds, *Power through Prayer*, 7.

## Chapter 7

1. Leona Choy, *Andrew and Emma Murray: An Intimate Portrait of Their Marriage and Ministry* (Winchester, Va.: Golden Morning Publishing, 2000), 89.

2. Ibid., 85–90.

3. Andrew Murray, *The Two Covenants* (Fort Washington, Pa.: Christian Literature Crusade, 1974), 73.

4. Ibid., 74–75.

5. Ibid., 79.

6. Ibid., 34.

7. Ibid., 114.

8. Ibid., 78.

9. Andrew Murray, *Divine Healing* (New Kensington, Pa.: Whitaker House, 1982), 85ff.

10. Murray, *Two Covenants*, 74.

11. Andrew Murray, *The Blood of the Cross* (Springdale, Pa.: Whitaker House, 1981), 59.

12. Andrew Murray, *With Christ in the School of Prayer* (Springdale, Pa.: Whitaker House, 1982), 93.

13. Murray, *Divine Healing*, 63. Used by permission of the publisher, Whitaker House.

14. Choy, *Andrew and Emma Murray*, 109–110.

15. Murray, *With Christ in the School of Prayer*, 89, 92, 94.

16. Murray, *Blood of the Cross*, 55–56.

17. Murray, *With Christ in the School of Prayer*, 218–219.

18. Howard and Geraldine Taylor, *Hudson Taylor's Spiritual Secret* (Chicago: Moody Press, 1932), 236.

19. Murray, *With Christ in the School of Prayer*, 81.

20. Ibid., 85–86.

21. Murray, *Divine Healing*, 36–37. Used by permission of the publisher, Whitaker House.

22. Murray, *With Christ in the School of Prayer*, 222; see also 83.

23. Murray, *Divine Healing*, 36. Used by permission of the publisher, Whitaker House.

24. Choy, *Andrew and Emma Murray*, 32.

25. Andrew Murray, *God's Best Secrets* (Grand Rapids: Zondervan, 1971), 12 November. But it must be stressed that Murray asserts the work of the Spirit of God is "no blind force." Andrew Murray, *The Inner Life* (Springdale, Pa.: Whitaker House, 1984), 115. Rather, determination in prayer, affirms Andrew Murray, will make "the morning watch itself a mighty force in strengthening our character and giving us boldness to resist self-indulgence." Murray, *Inner Life*, 11.

26. Murray, *With Christ in the School of Prayer*, 119.

27. Ibid., 117; see also 178.

28. Murray, *Divine Healing*, 13. Used by permission of the publisher, Whitaker House.

29. Ibid., 73–74.

30. Murray, *With Christ in the School of Prayer,* 82; see also 215ff.

31. William M. Douglas, *Andrew Murray and His Message* (Grand Rapids: Baker Book House, 1981), 330.

32. Ibid., 23; see also 114.

33. Andrew Murray, *The Prayer Life* (Basingstoke, UK: Marshall, Morgan, & Scott, 1968), 18.

34. Murray, *Divine Healing,* 45. Used by permission of the publisher, Whitaker House.

35. Ibid., 121.

36. Ibid., 45, 71.

37. Ibid., 69–70.

38. Ibid., 107–108.

39. Ibid., 114–115.

40. Ibid., 62.

41. Ibid., 18.

42. Choy, *Andrew and Emma Murray,* 155.

43. Murray, *Divine Healing,* 128. Though he sometimes received treatment from a doctor, Murray likewise advised that healing by a physician misses the greater blessing: "The healing which is wrought by our Lord Jesus brings with it and leaves behind it more real blessing than the healing which is obtained through physicians." Murray, *Divine Healing,* 20. Used by permission of the publisher, Whitaker House.

44. J. DuPlessis, *The Life of Andrew Murray of South Africa* (London: Marshall Brothers, 1919), 347.

45. Murray, *Divine Healing,* 52. Used by permission of the publisher, Whitaker House.

46. Ibid., 52–53.

47. Ibid., 133–134 (italics mine).

48. Murray, *Blood of the Cross,* 78.

49. Murray, *Prayer Life,* 18.

50. Andrew Murray, "Faith Counting on the Power of God," *Triumphs of Faith,* November 1934, 243.

51. Murray, *Key to the Missionary Problem,* 107.

52. Murray, *Blood of the Cross,* 60.

53. Andrew Murray, *Living the New Life* (Springdale, Pa.: Whitaker House, 1982), 139.

## Chapter 8

1. A. E. Thompson, *A. B. Simpson: His Life and Work* (Harrisburg, Pa.: Christian Publications, 1960), 120.

2. A. W. Tozer, *Wingspread* (Harrisburg, Pa.: Christian Publications, 1943), 103.

3. Robert L. Niklaus, John S. Sawin and Samuel J. Stoesz, *All for Jesus* (Camp Hill, Pa.: Christian Publications, 1986), 11.

4. Ibid., 51.

5. Both were raised in a formal Reformed tradition. Both experienced the dynamic, sanctifying empowering of the Holy Spirit. Both were dramatically and miraculously healed and published books on healing the same year, teaching many of the same concepts even though they had not met at that time.

6. A. B. Simpson, *The Land of Promise* (Harrisburg, Pa.: Christian Publications, 1969), 85.

7. A. B. Simpson, *The Highest Christian Life* (Harrisburg, Pa.: Christian Publications, 1966), 31.

8. Ibid., 86.

9. A. B. Simpson, *The Gentle Love of the Spirit* (Camp Hill, Pa.: Christian Publications, 1983), 118–119.

10. A. B. Simpson, *Days of Heaven on Earth* (Camp Hill, Pa.: Christian Publications, 1984), 6 October.

11. Ibid.

12. A. B. Simpson, *Christ in the Bible* (Camp Hill, Pa.: Christian Publications, 1992), vol. 6, 206.

13. A. B. Simpson, *Seeing the Invisible* (Camp Hill, Pa.: Christian Publications, 1994), 35. Unlike some modern teachers, Simpson carefully spells out that God's words, not man's, have creative power. God does the creating as a believer speaks in faith.

14. A. B. Simpson, *Triumphs of Faith*, November 1921, 253.

15. She advised, "Discouragement is the devil's visiting card, and that if we receive his card, the devil himself will come along after it." Carrie Judd Montgomery, *Secrets of Victory* (Oakland, Calif.: Triumphs of Faith, 1921), 66.

16. Simpson, *Christ in the Bible*, vol. 4, 247.

17. Simpson, *Seeing the Invisible*, 114–115.

18. Ibid., 33, 62, 129–130.

19. A. B. Simpson, *The Gospel of Healing* (Harrisburg, Pa.: Christian Publications, 1915), 90.

20. Simpson, *Days of Heaven on Earth*, 17 November.

21. Simpson counseled, "The shallow nature lives in its impulses, its impressions, its intuitions, its instincts and very largely in its surroundings. The profound character looks beyond all these and moves steadily on. . . . When God has deepened us, then He can give us His deeper truths, His profoundest secrets, His mightier trusts." Simpson, *Days of Heaven on Earth*, 3 December.

22. Simpson, *Gospel of Healing*, 160.

23. Tozer, *Wingspread*, 79.

24. Ibid. For Simpson's full testimony of healing, see also Simpson, *Gospel of Healing*, 153–172.

25. Simpson, *Gospel of Healing*, 161.

26. A. B. Simpson, *The Lord for the Body* (Camp Hill, Pa.: Christian Publications, 1996), 102, 103, 110–111.

27. Simpson, *Days of Heaven on Earth*, 18 June.

28. A. B. Simpson, "God's Voice in Sickness," *Triumphs of Faith*, July 1902, 164.

29. A. B. Simpson, *The Old Faith and the New Gospels* (Harrisburg, Pa.: Christian Publications, 1966), 60.

30. A. B. Simpson, "Two Stages of Divine Healing," *Alliance Weekly*, 28 January 1953, 5.

31. Simpson, *Lord for the Body*, 123–124.

32. A. B. Simpson, *Christ for the Body* (Nyack, N.Y.: Christian and Missionary Alliance, n.d.).

33. A. B. Simpson, *How to Receive Divine Healing* (Harrisburg, Pa.: Christian Publications, n.d.), 12.

34. Tozer, *Wingspread*, 127–128.

35. Simpson, *Gospel of Healing*, 88–90.

36. Tozer, *Wingspread*, 135.

37. Simpson, *Days of Heaven on Earth*, 20 October.

38. Simpson, *Seeing the Invisible*, 177.

39. "Grace's Consummation," *Alliance Weekly*, 8 December 1945, 423.

40. Simpson gave this illustration: "When an observatory is about to be built, the site selected is always on some high mountain. The aim is to find a place where there is a clear, unobstructed view of the heavens. Similarly, faith requires for its heavenly vision the highlands of holiness and separation, the pure sky of a consecrated life." A. B. Simpson, *A Larger Christian Life* (Camp Hill, Pa.: Christian Publications, 1988), 12–13.

41. A. B. Simpson, *Danger Lines in the Deeper Life* (Camp Hill, Pa.: Christian Publications, 1991), 101.

42. Simpson, *Seeing the Invisible*, 36.

43. Simpson, *Larger Christian Life*, 19.

44. Simpson, *Gospel of Healing*, 89.

45. A. B. Simpson, *The Fourfold Gospel* (Harrisburg, Pa.: Christian Publications, n.d.), 62.

46. *Hymns of the Christian Life* (Harrisburg, Pa.: Christian Publications, 1978), 248.

## Chapter 9

1. David W. Lambert, *Oswald Chambers* (Minneapolis: Bethany House, 1997), 123.

2. David McCasland, *Oswald Chambers: Abandoned to God* (Grand Rapids: Discovery House Publishers, 1993), back cover.

3. Ibid., 188–189.

4. Ibid., 157.

5. Ibid., 236.

6. Oswald Chambers, *Studies in the Sermon on the Mount* (Grand Rapids: Discovery House, 1995), 59.

7. Oswald Chambers, *Still Higher for His Highest* (Grand Rapids: Zondervan, 1970), 69.

8. Ibid., 20.

9. Oswald Chambers, *Daily Thoughts for Disciples* (Grand Rapids: Discovery House, 1994), 7 November.

10. McCasland, *Oswald Chambers*, 191.

11. Biddy Chambers, ed., *Oswald Chambers: His Life and Work* (London: Simpkin Marshall, 1933), 75.

12. McCasland, *Oswald Chambers*, 18.

13. Ibid., 147.

14. Ibid., 147, 189.

15. Ibid., 147–148.

16. Ibid., 102.

17. Oswald Chambers, *My Utmost for His Highest* (New York: Dodd, Mead, 1935, 1965), 146.

18. Ibid., 162, 279.

19. Ibid., 78, 322.

20. Oswald Chambers, *The Place of Help* (Grand Rapids: Discovery House Publishers, 1935, 1989), 91.

21. Chambers, *My Utmost for His Highest*, 221.

22. Chambers, *Daily Thoughts for Disciples*, 20 April.

23. Chambers, *My Utmost for His Highest*, 150.

24. Oswald Chambers, *The Psychology of Redemption* (London: Marshall, Morgan, & Scott, 1930, 1963), 68.

25. Ibid., 66–67.

26. Chambers, *My Utmost for His Highest*, 162.

27. Ibid., 155, 222.

28. B. Chambers, *Oswald Chambers*, 152–153.

29. McCasland, *Oswald Chambers*, 52–53.

30. Chambers, *My Utmost for His Highest*, 222.

31. B. Chambers, *Oswald Chambers*, 95.

32. Ibid.; McCasland, *Oswald Chambers*, 141.

33. B. Chambers, *Oswald Chambers*, 52.

34. Chambers, *Psychology of Redemption*, 20.

35. Chambers, *My Utmost for His Highest*, 304.

36. Ibid., 304.

37. McCasland, *Oswald Chambers*, 57.

38. Chambers, *My Utmost for His Highest*, 80.

39. B. Chambers, *Oswald Chambers*, 152.

40. Oswald Chambers, *Biblical Psychology* (Grand Rapids: Discovery House Publishers, 1962, 1995), 146.

41. Ibid., 200.

42. Ibid.

43. Ibid., 145.

44. B. Chambers, *Oswald Chambers*, 46.

45. McCasland, *Oswald Chambers*, 75.

46. Chambers, *My Utmost for His Highest*, 60.

47. Chambers, *Place of Help*, 160; *My Utmost for His Highest*, 81.

48. Chambers, *Place of Help*, 49.
49. Chambers, *My Utmost for His Highest*, 81.
50. Chambers, *Place of Help*, 210.
51. Ibid., 63.
52. B. Chambers, *Oswald Chambers*, 414. See McCasland, *Oswald Chambers*, 255–265 for the full story.
53. McCasland, *Oswald Chambers*, 262.
54. Ibid., 263–264.
55. Ibid., 18–19.

## Chapter 10

1. Elisabeth Elliot, *A Chance to Die: The Life and Legacy of Amy Carmichael* (Old Tappan, N.J.: Fleming H. Revell, 1987), 54.
2. For the full story, see Frank Houghton, *Amy Carmichael of Dohnavur* (Fort Washington, Pa.: Christian Literature Crusade, n.d.), 43–62; Elliot, *Chance to Die*, 51–64.
3. Elliott, *Chance to Die*, 89–90, 99, 168, 181, 193, 210, 235, 253, 276, 292–293.
4. Ibid., 85.
5. Ibid., 88–89.
6. Amy Carmichael, *Thou Givest . . . They Gather* (Fort Washington, Pa.: Christian Literature Crusade, 1958), 110.
7. Houghton, *Amy Carmichael of Dohnavur*, 118, 137; Elliot, *Chance to Die*, 181.
8. Amy Carmichael, *If* (Grand Rapids: Zondervan, 1980), part 2.
9. Carmichael, *Thou Givest*, 110.
10. Amy Carmichael, *You Are my Hiding Place*, arranged by David Hazard (Minneapolis: Bethany House, 1991), 44.
11. Elliot, *Chance to Die*, 98.
12. Ibid., 229.
13. Ibid., 117ff.
14. Ibid., 227.
15. Carmichael, *If*, part 2.
16. Houghton, *Amy Carmichael of Dohnavur*, 43, 45, 50, 74.
17. She gleaned this concept from one of her favorite mystical writers, Julian of Norwich. See Amy Carmichael, *Rose from Brier* (Fort Washington, Pa.: Christian Literature Crusade, 1933, 1971), 70. See also Elliot, *Chance to Die*, 253.
18. Elliot, *Chance to Die*, 100.
19. Ibid.
20. Carmichael, *Thou Givest*, 9; see also 12–14, 16. Carmichael added, "This special word may be given through another child of God" (14).
21. Amy Carmichael, *Raj, Brigand Chief* (Springfield, Mo.: Gospel Publishing House, 1962), 7–14; see also Elliot, *Chance to Die*, 259–260.
22. Elliot, *Chance to Die*, 253.

23. Houghton, *Amy Carmichael of Dohnavur,* 45.

24. Elliot, *Chance to Die,* 92.

25. Houghton, *Amy Carmichael of Dohnavur,* 67–69; Elliot, *Chance to Die,* 90–93.

26. She wrote a poem by this title. See Amy Carmichael, "Age-Long Minute," *Mountain Breezes: The Collected Poems of Amy Carmichael* (Fort Washington, Pa.: Christian Literature Crusade, 1999), 299. See also Carmichael, *Thou Givest,* 40; Elliot, *Chance to Die,* 278.

27. Elliot, *Chance to Die,* 276–279.

28. Carmichael, *If,* part 2.

29. Houghton, *Amy Carmichael of Dohnavur,* 75.

30. Elliot, *Chance to Die,* 253.

31. Amy Carmichael, *Gold Cord* (Fort Washington, Pa.: Christian Literature Crusade, n.d.), 360.

32. Elliot, *Chance to Die,* 220.

33. Ibid., 220.

34. Ibid., 55.

35. Ibid., 220.

36. Carmichael, *Rose from Brier,* 111.

37. Ibid., 28.

38. Elliott, *Chance to Die,* 263–264.

39. Ibid., 254.

40. Ibid., 251.

41. Ibid., 235–236.

42. According to Church history, Polycarp was condemned to death for his faith and was burned at the stake. However, he was not consumed in the fire but remained alive, unharmed. So the soldiers finally killed him by stabbing him through with a sword. Blood gushed out and extinguished the fire.

43. Carmichael, *Raj,* 54, 58–59; see also Elliott, *Chance to Die,* 261.

44. Carmichael, *If,* part 2.

45. Carmichael, *If,* parts 3, 7.

## Chapter 11

1. Many of these stories come from MacMillan's personal diary and memories from his students, recounted when he was a professor at the Missionary Training Institute, Nyack, New York (now Nyack College). For a fuller account of these stories, see my book *A Believer with Authority: The Life and Message of John A. MacMillan* (Camp Hill, Pa.: Christian Publications, 2001). Material in this chapter has been adapted from the book by permission of Christian Publications.

2. King, *Believer with Authority,* 96.

3. Ibid., 63.

4. Ibid., 93. This incident was recounted by one of MacMillan's former students, as described by MacMillan.

5. K. Neill Foster with Paul L. King, *Binding and Loosing: Exercising Authority over the Dark Powers* (Camp Hill, Pa.: Christian Publications, 1998), 247–248. Compiled from MacMillan's journal and from Jaffray's account as described by Tozer in *Let My People Go! The Life of Robert A. Jaffray* (Camp Hill, Pa.: Christian Publications, 1990), 43–49.

6. For a full description of this, see King, *Believer with Authority*, chs. 6, 7.

7. King, *Believer with Authority*, 61–62.

8. John A. MacMillan, *The Authority of the Believer* (Harrisburg, Pa.: Christian Publications, 1980).

9. John A. MacMillan, "The Authority of the Believer in the Ephesian Epistle: Part 6," *Alliance Weekly*, 20 February 1932, 116. Material from this series is used by permission of *Alliance Life*, formerly *The Alliance Weekly*, published by The Christian and Missionary Alliance.

10. John A. MacMillan, "The Authority of the Believer in the Ephesian Epistle: Part 7," *Alliance Weekly*, 27 February 1932, 133. Used by permission of *Alliance Life*.

11. John A. MacMillan, "The Authority of the Rod," *Alliance Weekly*, 18 May 1940, 314. Used by permission of *Alliance Life*.

12. "Shaming Our God," *Alliance Weekly*, 23 February 1946, 114; "Family Privileges," *Alliance Weekly*, 7 August 1937, 498.

13. "The Victory of God," *Alliance Weekly*, 22 April 1944, 210.

14. John A. MacMillan, "The Authority of the Believer in the Ephesian Epistle: Part 3," *Alliance Weekly*, 23 January 1932, 61.

15. King, *Believer with Authority*, 38–39.

16. "Raging Chariots," *Alliance Weekly*, 15 May 1937, 307; see also *Full Gospel Adult Sunday School Quarterly*, 27 December 1936, 40.

17. See King, *Believer with Authority*, 90.

18. "The Family Altar," *Alliance Weekly*, 5 May 1945, 130; *Full Gospel Adult Sunday School Quarterly*, 23 December 1934, 36.

19. King, *Believer with Authority*, 63–64.

20. John A. MacMillan, *Encounter with Darkness* (Harrisburg, Pa.: Christian Publications, 1980), 55–56.

21. MacMillan, "Ephesian Epistle: Part 6," 116. Used by permission of *Alliance Life*.

22. Ibid. MacMillan also related that "similar cases occurred in the Girls' School." In one situation the girls were fighting, and the instigator continued to scream, even after being separated from the others. Under his breath, MacMillan rebuked evil spirits and took authority in the name of Jesus. The girl immediately stopped shrieking and became quiet.

23. Ibid. See also King, *Believer with Authority*, 94–95.

24. Ibid. In one of those situations, a woman on a boat trip became highly agitated and began manifesting demonic symptoms. MacMillan again quietly exercised authority, binding the spirits in the name of Jesus Christ. The woman became still and the attack did not return.

25. "Cleansed Within," *Alliance Weekly*, 14 January 1939, 19.

26. "Go Forward!" *Alliance Weekly*, 11 May 1946, 290.

27. MacMillan, "Ephesian Epistle: Part 7," 133. Used by permission of *Alliance Life*.

28. For a description of the teaching and practice of binding and loosing among evangelical leaders throughout Church history, see Foster and King, *Binding and Loosing*.

29. King, *Believer with Authority*, 65–66. For example, when I was a pastor, one of my church members came to me saying that he did not need to give up smoking. His justification was that he had bound and rebuked a spirit of nicotine, so that the cigarettes were now free of demonic influence. Obviously, he was rationalizing rather than dealing with the real issues of his addiction and the pleasures he derived from smoking.

30. "All Authority," *Alliance Weekly*, 2 March 1940, 130.

31. John A. MacMillan, "The Authority of the Intercessor," *Alliance Weekly*, 23 May 1936, 326–327. Used by permission of *Alliance Life*. He asserted further, "It is a good exercise to '*say*' aloud to our difficulties, as we kneel in prayer, 'Be thou removed.' The *saying*, if in faith in the name of the Lord, will cause a stirring at the roots; and as we keep steadfastly holding to God and *saying*, the time will come when the tree which has been opposing, or the mountain which has been hindering, will quietly move into the sea of oblivion." *Full Gospel Adult Sunday School Quarterly*, 3 May 1936, 17; see also *Full Gospel Adult Sunday School Quarterly*, 13 May 1934, 19.

32. King, *Believer with Authority*, 231.

33. *Full Gospel Adult Sunday School Quarterly*, 22 November 1942, 25.

34. "The Cooperating Spirit," *Alliance Weekly*, 4 May 1936, 275.

35. See King, *Believer with Authority*, ch. 8, for this entire incident.

36. MacMillan's diary, as cited in King, *Believer with Authority*, 101.

37. Ibid., 102.

38. Ibid.

39. *Full Gospel Adult Sunday School Quarterly*, 23 November 1941, 24.

40. MacMillan later wrote, "Everything that comes may not seem to be of God, but our attitude of thanksgiving towards Him must continue, even when we discern that some things that have been permitted to touch us are as definitely from the enemy as were the afflictions of Job. Such things are for our training spiritually, and under them it is ours to maintain a heart that dwells in praise before the Lord." *Full Gospel Adult Sunday School Quarterly*, 23 November 1941, 25.

41. "The Mysteries of Prayer," *Alliance Weekly*, 20 May 1944, 242. Quoting Luke 10:19 on the believer's authority, MacMillan commented, obviously alluding to Isabel, "This is the normal condition of the ministry of the missionary; when trouble is stirred up by the enemy, the servant of God has the right to appeal to this promise of his Lord. Only when the glory of the Lord is better served by resisting 'unto blood,' it is superseded; then it may be that the glory of God is promoted by death, rather than by life. But to the trusting and obedient soul these things will be plain when the time comes." *Full Gospel Adult Sunday School Quarterly*, 7 May 1939, 19.

42. As we have seen throughout this book, frequently God's models of faith have been tried in the fire, bereaved of their loved ones—George Müller lost a son, Hudson Taylor lost four children under the age of 10 and his wife when he was 33 years old. Phoebe Palmer, Hannah Whitall Smith, E. M. Bounds, A. B. Simpson—all lost children as well. These men and women persevered with strong faith in spite of their losses. The healing ministries of F. F. Bosworth and Smith Wigglesworth actually increased after the deaths of their loved ones.

43. "Fasting as an Aid to Prayer," *Alliance Weekly*, 4 March 1950, 130; MacMillan, *Authority of the Believer*, 96.

44. "A United World," *Alliance Weekly*, 14 September 1946, 578.

45. "Christ is at the right hand of God, the very seat of all authority, and united with Him are His believing saints. To them is given to share His authority even here and now, to the limit of their faith and their spiritual comprehension. But such is the blinding power of the enemy that few indeed have any conception of the gracious purpose of God in this regard. . . . Herein lies much of the weakness of the Church." John A. MacMillan, "Israel's Night of Remembrance," *Alliance Weekly*, 22 November 1941, 754. His commentary on the Church in the 1940s could well be applied to the Church today: "A united, instructed and praying church could control the power of the air. But the church is not united, neither is it instructed in the matters of heavenly warfare. Nor yet is it a praying church. A little flock of intercessors bears the burden of supplication for 'kings and for all that are in authority.'" "The Power of the Air," *Alliance Weekly*, 28 August 1948, 546.

46. *Full Gospel Adult Sunday School Quarterly*, 3 May 1936, 17.

47. John A. MacMillan, "The Authority of the Believer in the Ephesian Epistle: Part 1," *Alliance Weekly*, 9 January 1932, 22.

## Chapter 12

1. A. W. Tozer, *The Divine Conquest* (Old Tappan, N.J.: Revell, 1950), 11.

2. James L. Snyder, *In Pursuit of God: The Life of A. W. Tozer* (Camp Hill, Pa.: Christian Publications, 1991), 121–122. Reprinted from James L. Snyder, *In Pursuit of God: The Life of A. W. Tozer,* copyright © 1991 Christian Publications. Used by permission of Christian Publications, 800.233.4443, <www.christianpublications.com>.

3. A. W. Tozer, *The Pursuit of God* (Harrisburg, Pa.: Christian Publications, 1948), 7–8. Reprinted from A. W. Tozer, *The Pursuit of God,* copyright © 1982, 1993 Christian Publications. Used by permission of Christian Publications, 800.233.4443, <www.christianpublications.com>.

4. Snyder, *In Pursuit of God,* 124–125. Used by permission of Christian Publications.

5. David J. Fant, *A. W. Tozer: A Twentieth-Century Prophet* (Harrisburg, Pa.: Christian Publications, 1964), 147.

6. Tozer, *Pursuit of God,* 20. Used by permission of Christian Publications.

7. Snyder, *In Pursuit of God*, 2. Used by permission of Christian Publications.

8. A. W. Tozer, *Worship: The Missing Jewel* (Camp Hill, Pa.: Christian Publications, 1992).

9. Snyder, *In Pursuit of God*, 149. Used by permission of Christian Publications. See also Tozer, *Worship*, 4–6.

10. A. W. Tozer, *The Root of the Righteous* (Harrisburg, Pa.: Christian Publications, 1955), 92.

11. A. W. Tozer, *Born after Midnight* (Camp Hill, Pa.: Christian Publications, 1989), 125.

12. Snyder, *In Pursuit of God*, 106. Used by permission of Christian Publications.

13. Ibid., 148.

14. Ibid., 161. Used by permission of Christian Publications.

15. Ibid., 193. Used by permission of Christian Publications.

16. Tozer, *Pursuit of God*, 108. Used by permission of Christian Publications.

17. Snyder, *In Pursuit of God*, 54–55.

18. A. W. Tozer, *I Talk Back to the Devil* (Camp Hill, Pa.: Christian Publications, 1990), 26.

19. A. W. Tozer, *The Price of Neglect* (Camp Hill, Pa.: Christian Publications, 1991), 49.

20. A. W. Tozer, *We Travel an Appointed Way* (Camp Hill, Pa.: Christian Publications, 1988), 4.

21. Snyder, *In Pursuit of God*, 123. Used by permission of Christian Publications.

22. A. W. Tozer, *God Tells the Man Who Cares* (Camp Hill, Pa.: Christian Publications, 1992), 105.

23. Snyder, *In Pursuit of God*, 96. Used by permission of Christian Publications.

24. Ibid., 209. Used by permission of Christian Publications.

25. Tozer, *Pursuit of God*, 116. Used by permission of Christian Publications.

26. Fant, 21.

27. Ibid., 47–48.

28. Snyder, *In Pursuit of God*, 70. Used by permission of Christian Publications.

29. A. W. Tozer, *Five Vows of Spiritual Power* (Camp Hill, Pa.: Christian Publications, 1996), n.p. Reprinted from A. W. Tozer, *Five Vows of Spiritual Power*, copyright © 1996 Christian Publications. Used by permission of Christian Publications, 800.233.4443, <www.christianpublications.com>.

30. A. W. Tozer, *That Incredible Christian* (Harrisburg, Pa.: Christian Publications, 1964), 59, 61.

31. A. W. Tozer, *The Early Tozer: A Word in Season* (Camp Hill, Pa.: Christian Publications, 1997), 30.

32. Snyder, *In Pursuit of God*, 104.

33. A. W. Tozer, *Tragedy in the Church: The Missing Gifts* (Harrisburg, Pa.: Christian Publications, 1978).

34. Ibid., 132. Used by permission of Christian Publications.

35. A. W. Tozer, *Of God and Men* (Harrisburg, Pa.: Christian Publications, 1960), 54.

36. Ibid., 57. See also A. W. Tozer, *Jesus, Author of Our Faith* (Camp Hill, Pa.: Christian Publications, 1988), 5–6; A. W. Tozer, *Faith beyond Reason* (Camp Hill, Pa.: Christian Publications, 1989), 34.

37. Tozer, *Jesus, Author of Our Faith*, 6.

38. Tozer, *Pursuit of God*, 90–91. Used by permission of Christian Publications.

39. Tozer, *Faith beyond Reason*, 36; see also 35–42; Tozer, *Jesus, Author of Our Faith*, 9–12.

40. A. W. Tozer, *Born after Midnight*, 44.

41. Snyder, *In Pursuit of God*, 154. Used by permission of Christian Publications.

42. Ibid., 156. Used by permission of Christian Publications.

43. Tozer, *Pursuit of God*, 98. Used by permission of Christian Publications.

# Index

**Paul L. King**, ordained by The Christian and Missionary Alliance (CMA), has a Doctor of Theology (University of South Africa, 2002) and Doctor of Ministry (Oral Roberts University, 2000). As a professor at Oral Roberts University he oversees the ORU Bible Institute program and teaches seminars on healing and on ministry and leadership development internationally. He is an expert on nineteenth- and early-twentieth-century classic leaders of faith, healing and holiness. He has researched and edited *Classic Christianity*, an e-mail magazine, and has published numerous articles in popular and academic journals on these classic leaders and their teachings. King bridges the evangelical and charismatic communities. As a CMA minister he serves the largely noncharismatic evangelical community, while on the faculty of ORU he serves the charismatic community. King is the coauthor of *Binding and Loosing: Exercising Authority over the Dark Powers* and author of *A Believer with Authority: The Life and Message of John A. MacMillan.*